Revolution and International System

REVOLUTION
and International System

Kyung-Won Kim

Associate Professor of Political Science

New York University

New York: NEW YORK UNIVERSITY PRESS
London: UNIVERSITY OF LONDON PRESS, LTD

1970

Excerpts from R. R. Palmer's *The Age of the Democratic Revolution: A Political History of Europe and America 1760-1800*, Volume II: *The Struggle,* © 1964 by Princeton University Press. Reprinted by permission of Princeton University Press.

Excerpts from Morton Kaplan's *System and Process in International Politics,* © 1957 by John Wiley & Sons, Inc. Reprinted by permission of John Wiley & Sons, Inc.

Preface

The extent of my indebtedness to the published sources from which I have derived help and insight, even when I am critical of them, will be apparent to whoever reads this book.

My obligations to individuals are still heavier. I owe special thanks to the following for their comments on earlier drafts of the book: Professor Henry Kissinger, then of Harvard University, Professor Douglas Verney of York University (Toronto, Canada), Professor I. William Zartman of New York University, and above all, Professor Stanley Hoffman of Harvard University. For the errors of fact and interpretation, I alone am responsible.

I also wish to thank the Canada Council for a research grant which allowed me to concentrate on the completion of this volume free from normal duties of teaching.

Contents

Introduction

This book is an analysis of the impact of the French Revolution on the international relations of the time. In writing it, I have had mainly three concerns: historical, practical, and theoretical.

The historical concern is the most obvious one, and perhaps the least important. It is least important because this book is not primarily a historical monograph, although the theoretical analysis contained in it draws heavily upon historical data. Also, I hesitate to put forward my historical concern because, despite my instinctive suspicion that the forces unleashed by the French Revolution are still very much upon us, I am only too painfully aware of the risks involved in making broad generalizations regarding any secular historical trend. It is tempting indeed to say that the democratic impulse which lay behind the French Revolution and eventually destroyed the classical international system of the eighteenth century constitutes still the essence of our international dilemma, perhaps even more so than ever before. But on the other hand, I am no less anxious to avoid the kind of historicism which such observation of a secular historical trend would certainly involve if it were suggested as anything more than a hunch. Caught, therefore, between the instinctive inclination to generalize about what seems to me a clearly discernible historical trend, and the equally strong desire to avoid historical determinism, I wish only to suggest this possibility of historical interpretation, and hope that with enough concrete research we may eventually establish more secure ground for confirming or rejecting it.

My second concern is practical. Obviously we live in a revolutionary age, and the sources of international instability in our own time may well be similar to those of the period of the French Revolution. The problems of conservative statesmanship, too, may well be the same now as then. The temptation, therefore, is quite strong to draw an analogy and derive from the previous experience practical lessons for our own time. But here again I have decided not to push the analogy explicitly. Analogy is one of the most primitive forms of historical thought, and my impression is that it has given rise to more erroneous judgments on matters of practical concern than most other forms. "Munich" has often been cited indiscriminately, confusing the real issues of the situation rather than clarifying them. I doubt, therefore, if a historical analogy is really helpful for practical solutions of contemporary problems.

This skepticism, however, does not mean rejection of comparative analysis. It is indeed my belief in the value of comparative analysis that led me to this study. And this brings me to my final and primary concern in this work which is essentially theoretical.

The theory of international relations is in its infancy, as E. H. Carr said of the science of international relations almost three decades ago![1] Despite a flood of self-consciously theoretical works in the field, it is doubtful if anyone would be so bold as to deny the extreme immaturity of international-relations theory.

What is curious, however, is not so much the backwardness of theoretical work, but rather the manner in which belated consciousness of theoretical poverty has tended to take away from contemporary scholarship even that which the study of international relations did possess previously, namely a firm grounding in history. Anxious to develop "scientific" theories of international relations, scholars in the field have tended to minimize the value of historical data. There appear to be three reasons for this trend. One is inherent in the nature of diplomatic history, which is apparently the branch of history closest to international relations. As Max Beloff observed some time ago, "Of all forms of history, diplomatic history is the least profitable."[2]

Diplomatic history, as compared with social history or history of ideas, tends to be mainly factual and particularistic and to contain too many apparently "accidental" elements. It is no wonder that, with the recent trend toward more sociologically oriented historiography, the best minds in the discipline of history itself have on the whole shied away from the diplomatic branch.

Second, related to the first but separate from it, is the fact that the basic theoretical framework within which historical data tended to be subsumed, that is, the so-called "realist" analysis, is pretty well rejected as a theory of international relations, at least among those who have been most responsible for expanding the frontiers of research in the field. No longer passionately involved in the realist-idealist controversy, most of us tend to throw out the basic data on which the debate rested as well as rejecting its mode of analysis. This is why, despite the lip service paid to history as "the great laboratory"[3] of international relations, many theorists have yet to get inside the lab and work in it. We have rejected the "realist" analysis of international relations which interpreted diplomatic history in terms of the simplified and monistic concept of power, but we have not yet learned how otherwise to make use of history in the theoretical analysis of international relations.

A third reason for the general tendency to depreciate history, I would also suggest, may lie in the fact that most of the theoretically oriented researches and writings are done by American scholars. This may have two unintended effects. One is a predominantly policy-oriented preoccupation with contemporary problems, which is quite understandable in the light of America's pragmatic tradition and its contemporary world position. The second is more subtle but perhaps more crucial. It is that American social scientists, by virtue of the almost unique nature of America's own historical experience,[4] tend to minimize the relevance of history for the understanding of the present. It is no accident, for instance, that voting studies tend to yield more dividends in the case of American politics than they do with respect to older societies. By the same token, American students of international relations are more likely to concentrate on self-consciously scientific studies than on historical research. If statistics, simulation, and systems analysis seem to dominate the current research scene, it may well be a peculiarly American phenomenon.

I have thus undertaken this study to consciously explore possible ways of using history. My primary purpose was not to write history as such, but to make use of historical data in an effort to gain a theoretical understanding of the nature of international relations. This book, therefore, is essentially an exercise in the theory of international relations. As the concluding chapter will show, I am concerned with the impact of the French Revolution on the international relations of the time only insofar as such impact may be analyzed to reveal the nature of the interaction process between a major political revolution and the existing international system in general. The analysis of one historical case, however careful and detailed, could not by itself establish the validity of any generalization which may be suggested by it. In this regard, the value of history for theory is basically negative. The validity of the latter may be disproved but cannot be conclusively established by the evidence of the former. What a careful and detailed analysis of a given historical case can yield is a set of insights which in principle can be turned into meaningful generalizations through subsequent studies of analogous historical situations. To accomplish such a task, a case study must of course rest on a more or less explicit theoretical framework. In other words, if the conclusions of a case study are to have, at least in principle, greater validity than is to be found in most straightforward historical monographs, the first requirement is that the study start from a set of conditions which define and limit the possible area of its applicability.

The first presupposition for the book, then, is that a theory of international relations can only be a set of generalizations about the whole of international relations and not merely its parts. The much touted "level-of-analysis problem" aside,[5] the fact remains that there is a difference between a theory of foreign policy as such and a theory of international relations. One does not produce the latter by piling up theories of foreign policy for the rather obvious reason that there are aspects to international relations which would be left out of even a thorough account of foreign policies—unless such an account were based upon a theory of international relations to begin with. This is why I find the notion of international system a very useful one, and I have chosen to concentrate on the impact of the French Revolution on the international system of the time rather than deal with the foreign policies of this or that country in the manner of traditional diplomatic history.

To be sure, there exists a good deal of confusion regarding the meaning of the concept of "international system," as a number of scholars have defined it differently to suit their individual needs and analytic purposes. The range of possible meanings varies all the way from Morton Kaplan's self-consciously scientific attempt at a rigorous and precise definition to Raymond Aron's rather flexible and also somewhat ambiguous definition.[6] To a conscientious graduate student preparing for doctoral examinations, such a variety of definitions can be a source of frustration, bewilderment, and disillusionment. Upon reflection, however, I believe one can detect behind all the conflicting definitions and assertions a convergence of similar and related interests and perspectives. I have in mind the often unstated but common assumption, basic to the notion of international system however it is defined, that the field of international relations possesses properties that are not necessarily entailed in the definition of its component elements. Now, the latter may be described as foreign policies of nation-states or merely classified as subsystemic. In any case, what those who are self-consciously scientific and others who would rather be concerned with historical and political substance than with scientific procedure have in common is, in using the term "international system," both schools of thought make two common assumptions. One is that there are certain crucial aspects to international relations as a whole that constitute constraining factors for foreign policies, and the second is that such constraining factors can be understood or analyzed better from the perspective of international relations as a whole than from any individual-actor-oriented point of view.

What, then, are such constraining factors? As I have implied that they are not inherent in the structure of subsystemic units, whether they are nation-states or city-states, the clear inference is that the relevant factors from the point of view of a theory of international relations are to be found in the nature of relations among the units comprising a system of international relations. To put it another way, essential variables of any given international system must have to do with the nature of the contextual relationship among existing component units or subsystems, although to assume this is not to rule out the role of domestic factors in the determination of foreign policies. On the contrary, as the conclusions of this study bear out most strongly, domestic factors tend to have the most decisive effect on foreign policies and indirectly on the shape of international systems as well. What the stress on systemic constraints implies is that a general theory of international relations, insofar as it is primarily a theory of international relations and not an explanation of foreign policy, must have its central focus in a model of international relations and incorporate subsystemic variables on the basis of propositions descriptive of systemic properties. By and large, then, it may be asserted that the use of the phrase "international system" is meaningful on two accounts. First, it means that the analyst using it is stressing the relation of forces, a phenomenon that is not inherent in any subsystemic structure as such but results from the coexistence of plural subsystems in a mutually interacting relationship. Second, it also means that the role of ideology, or totality of political and international aims and values, cannot be adequately assessed, insofar as international relations are concerned, except in the context of a mutual relationship among ideologies of component subsystemic units.[7] In contrast to comparative politics, a field in which ideology assumes significance by virtue of its substantive content, what is most decisive in the field of international relations is more often the nature of the relationship among ideologies of constituent units than the character of ideologies themselves.

To be more specific, the relation of forces may be of three definitive kinds: unipolar, bipolar, and multipolar. The definition of a given international system in terms of the relation of forces is determined by the number of dominant actors capable of affecting the distribution of power within the system, or at least in a position to do so negatively by losing their status as "dominant actors." The assumption behind such a classification is that the substance of interstate behavior would vary significantly with the number of dominant powers at any given historical period and within a region of regularly interacting states. What the exact pattern of interaction is in each type of international system is of course something that cannot be settled by definitions and deductions alone. It can be answered only by detailed research in the history of international relations. We can assume, however, without too much fear of being wrong, that the number of dominant powers in an international system would have a crucial bearing on the way states act or do not act toward each other.[8] There could be no serious objection, for instance, to the suggestion that a system dominated by one supreme power, as was the traditional order in East Asia, would exhibit forms of interaction among states that would be quite different from those expected to prevail in a multipolar system. By the same token, we can also assume that between bipolar (of two dominant powers) and multipolar (of three or more powers) systems there would be significant differences in the degree of complexity of calculation, the nature of risk, the requirement for orderly or predictable behavior, the need for coalition, and so on.

It is on the basis of this assumption that I have attempted in this book to analyze the impact of the French Revolution in terms of its effect on the bipolarization of the European system. The pattern of international relations preceding the Revolution, as the next chapter will show, depended to a large extent on the fact of multiple centers of power. The stabilization in Europe following the wars of religion coincided not accidentally with the transition from an essentially bipolar struggle to a multipolar competition. This is not to assert flatly that there is a kind of mechanical correlation between multipolarity of power and systemic stability, as some quantitatively oriented researchers tend to assume.[9] Stability of international relations is affected not only by more factors than the number of dominant powers in a given system, but also by the way in which such affecting factors interact with each power. Ecological variables no doubt condition the state of an international system as well as causing changes in it. All that is suggested here is that if we concentrate on the level of interstate actions and reactions, rather than environmental factors external to them, the number of dominant powers becomes one of the most important dimensions in the analysis of international systems.

The second dimension is ideology. The most important question here is: Does a given international system contain states committed to mutually conflicting conceptions of rights and obligations, pursuing antagonistic aims and visions, or not? It is possible to divide the history of international relations into two basic patterns, ideologically homogeneous and heterogeneous systems, on the basis of the answer to this question. The distinction, borrowed by Raymond Aron from a work of Panoyis Papaligouras,[10] rests on the assumption that an ideologically homogeneous system is likely to be more stable than a heterogeneous one. Having made such an assumption, however, we face the following questions: What is ideology? What is meant by homogeneity (and heterogeneity)? Why is one system more stable than the other?

The concept of ideology ranges all the way from a "science of ideas,"[11] the original notion, to "a configuraton of ideas and attitudes in which the elements are bound together by some form of constraint or functional interdependence,"[12] a psychologically oriented definition. For the present purpose, it is enough to use the concept of ideology as it is most commonly understood, namely to mean a more or less systematic body of ideas about politics and society. It is systematic in that an isolated notion, although it may be about political life, cannot constitue an ideology by itself unless it is at the same time linked to some far-reaching and more fundamental concepts and derivations from them. Thus normally an ideology contains not only particular conceptions of justice and political authority, but also certain assumptions about human nature and society as well. The degree to which an ideology is systematic depends of course on the explicitness of its conceptual formulation and the stage of its historical development. In any case, explicitly or implicitly, an ideology is fairly comprehensive in its overall conception. It may be denoted by the more ambitious term, world-view (*Weltanschauung*). An ideology is not merely a prescription for a better world. It is normally derived from a comprehensive view of what the world really is. An ideology, therefore, amounts to a set of assumptions without which the mass of concrete and therefore necessarily discrete facts would dissolve into (or remain as?) a meaningless chaos. In this sense, an ideological commitment may be viewed as an act of faith that enables the believer to confer upon (or discover in?) his world a degree of coherence which would be absent otherwise.

We are not, however, interested in an essentially metaphysical question which the concept of ideology suggests, namely: Is thought necessarily ideological in character? For the purposes of analysis attempted in this book, we do not even have to assume what Mannheim so confidently presumed—that thought is ideological and always socially derived.[13] Suspending our judgment on these more fundamental questions, we can formulate a working definition of ideology by making a distinction between it and a scientific form of thought. The crucial difference, admittedly a matter of degree since it does not imply an absolute, unbridgeable gap between the two, is that while scientific thought is intentionally only descriptive of what *is,* ideological thought necessarily advocates what *ought to be.* A political ideology, therefore, prescribes a particular conception of rights and obligations, and for those who accept it, it has the function of conferring legitimacy on a particular structure of power and society. Authority, which in essence is the noncoercive foundation of power in any political system, can thus be seen to be a product of ideology.

The relevance of the foregoing discussion for the analysis of international systems is twofold. First, in speaking of ideology, we mean primarily domestic ideology, simply because ideology, concerned as it is with legitimacy and authority, has been primarily domestic in its orientation. The object of its concern has been necessarily a political society, which an international system has not been. In fact, for most theoretical writers on politics from Plato to Pareto, the typical attitude regarding interstate relations has been either indifference or a matter-of-fact military orientation. Not even recent ideologies such as liberalism and socialism, which are more strongly concerned with international relations than traditional theories of politics, can be seriously considered as primarily international. Their international aspects are derived from their domestic concerns. Like other ideologies, they are basically principles of legitimacy, and as such are theories of domestic political life.

Second, by ideological homogeneity we mean compatible principles of legitimacy—conversely, by ideological heterogeneity, conflicting conceptions of political authority and obligation which are not only different from each other but mutually exclusive. Examples of the former are procapitalist liberalism and democratic socialism, or constitutionalist conservatism and liberalism. Examples of the latter are royalism versus republicanism, or capitalism versus communism. In the case of the former, coexistence does not present a great problem, since there is no wholesale challenge to the basic legitimacy of the existing constitutional structure, whereas in the case of heterogeneous ideologies, it is precisely such fundamental structures that are at stake. To be sure, ideological heterogeneity is a matter of degree. Also, in applying the concept to actual historical life, one should take care to avoid grafting a conceptual rigidity onto the historical reality, which is bound to be complex and changing. All that is suggested here is that international systems composed of ideologically heterogeneous actors are less stable and thus more prone to breakdown than homogeneous systems. One important purpose of this study is precisely to examine such a connection between ideological heterogeneity and instability of international relations. Or, more broadly, to pose—and answer—the queries: What are the conditions of international stability and instability? How and why does an international system break down?

The second assumption of this book, therefore, is that the international system that lasted from the end of the wars of religion to the French Revolution did indeed break down. On the basis of this assumption, the study proceeds to analyze the process of dissolution of the classical interstate system. Is the assumption of systemic breakdown, however, actually warranted? The answer will depend to a certain extent on the definition of "systemic breakdown" as well as the actual historical record. If the breakdown of an international system is taken to mean permanent and irreversible transformation of some kind, obviously there is room for disagreement concerning the impact of the French Revolution on international relations. If the concept of systemic breakdown is freed from implications of permanent historical transformation, on the other hand, it raises no great controversy to say that the classical international system of Europe broke down as a result of the French Revolution and its repercussions. It broke down enough so that it had to be consciously "restored." The system that was "restored" may have been in effect identical with the system that preceded the French Revolution in fundamental structural properties—but the fact remains that the Revolution succeeded in depriving the classical international relations of their basic stability.* As a result of the Revolution, international relations in Europe at the end of the eighteenth century were deprived of both ideological homogeneity and multipolarity of power, two characteristics which had characterized the relations among European states up to that time. My concern is to discover how such changes affected the general stability of international relations.

The possible payoff of the study is, then, twofold. First, the more direct result will be a set of answers to some specific questions, a set of answers which will be mainly applicable to the specific case at hand, namely, the breakdown of a classical balance-of-power system. Second, on a more theoretical level, it should be possible to arrive at a set of generalizations which, though limited by having been generated through a single case study, can nevertheless form the basis for further comparative analysis. The role of ideology, for instance, can be more sharply defined as a result of this study, and the definition applied elsewhere to discover the extent to which the insight gained from this particular analysis may be generalized into a universal theory. I suggest the second possibility most cautiously, not only because of the limited nature of this essay, but also, and more important, because I tend to be skeptical of unabashedly "general" theories. Without committing myself to the position that historical events are not amenable to generalization because of their uniqueness, a position that, if pushed to the extreme, becomes rather trivial, I do hold the view that for all practical purposes historical events—at least important and interesting ones—are almost always unrepeated and therefore

---

*This point is further developed in the next chapter.

unique in their rich fullness of detail. Thus one is more often than not forced to achieve the lofty aim of generalization only at the expense of relevence.[14] It is therefore advisable to keep one's feet firmly on the ground of history, particularly if one is temperamentally inclined toward theory as I believe I myself am.

Finally, a few words about the organization of the book. The following chapter is devoted to an analysis of the international system that preceded the French Revolution. The definition of the prerevolutionary international system then forms the starting point for subsequent chapters, each of which deals with a different phase in the process of interaction between the Revolution and the international system. Most chapters are divided into two parts, the first dealing with the historical record and the second attempting to squeeze theoretical dividends out of the historical analysis. The concluding chapter is an attempt to collect those theoretical dividends and cast them into the form of general hypotheses, which can then be used for subsequent studies along similar lines. The hypotheses of the last chapter are also tied together in a coherent manner to suggest at least a partial theory of international destabilization.

Notes

1. H. Carr, *The Twenty Years' Crisis, 1919–1939* (London, 1940), p. 1.
2. Max Beloff, *The Age of Absolutism: 1660–1815* (London, 1954), p. 28.
3. See, for instance, Morton A. Kaplan, *System and Process in International Politics* (New York, 1957). Although Kaplan opens his first chapter by calling history "the great laboratory within which international action occurs," it is hard to see in the rest of the book that Kaplan is working in that laboratory.
4. See Louis Hartz, *The Liberal Tradition in America: An Interpretation of American Political Thought Since the Revolution* (New York, 1955).
5. J. D. Singer, "The Level-of-Analysis Problem in International Relations," *World Politics*, Vol. XIV, No. 1 (Oct., 1961).
6. For Morton Kaplan's definition, see *op. cit.*, Part One, Chap. 2; for Raymond Aron's, see *Peace and War, A Theory of International Relations* translated by R. Howard and A. B. Fox (New York, 1967), Part One, Chap IV.

7. Obviously I have drawn heavily upon Raymond Aron's work, but, I believe, with some significant differences, as will become recognizable later in the book.

8. In this connection, Arthur Lee Burns offers a very interesting discussion. See *Of Powers and Their Politics, A Critique of Theoretical Approaches* (Englewood Cliffs, N. J., 1968), Chap. V, pp. 93–121.

9. See, for instance, J. David Singer and Melvin Small, "Alliance Aggregation and the Onset of War, 1815–1945," an article which is interestingly conceived but disappointing in its naïve and mechanical operationalization of complex and dynamic historical phenomena. *Quantitative International Politics, Insights and Evidence,* J. David Singer, ed. (New York, 1968), pp. 247–286.

10. Raymond Aron, *op. cit.,* p. 100.

11. Destutt de Tracy, *Eléments d'idéologie* (Bruxelles, 1826), p. 3.

12. Philip E. Converse, "The Nature of Beliefs Systems in Mass Publics," in David E. Apter, ed., *Ideology and Discontent* (New York, 1964).

13. Karl Mannheim, *Ideology and Utopia, An Introduction to the Sociology of Knowledge,* translated by Louis Wirth and Edward Shils (New York, 1936), Chap. II.

14. I have dealt elsewhere with this and other metatheoretical problems. "The Limits of Behavioral Explanation in Politics," *The Canadian Journal of Economics and Political Science,* Vol. XXXI, No. 3 (Aug., 1965).

Revolution and International System

I

The International System Under the *Ancien Régime*

The nineteenth-century German historian Leopold Ranke, despite his self-imposed obligation to write history exactly as it happened, once asserted that beyond the welter of events and personalities there exists that mystical "genius which always protects Europe from domination by any one-sided and violent tendency."[1] He might have added that the "genius" occasionally comes perilously close to failing his duty and plunging Europe into something far worse and more violent than "any one-sided . . . tendency"—certainly true of Europe during the wars of religion and again during the period of the French Revolution and Napoleonic wars. Between these two points, however, Europe indeed seemed to be protected by Ranke's mystical genius, which not only ensured diversity (multipolarity?) but also brought a degree of stability to the relations among sovereign states. It was as if the Americans' favorite self-congratulatory rhetoric about their federalism could be applied equally to the European family of territorial states, at least during the period later to be dubbed by admiring historians "the Age of Reason." In any case, the international system comprising the European states from the Treaty of Westphalia to the beginning of the French revolutionary wars in 1792 could be described, using the two dimensions singled out for analysis in the previous chapter, as multipolar in the distribution of power and homogeneous in cultural habits and political convictions.

Neither multipolarity of power nor ideological homogeneity

was so absolute as to be self-evident and beyond dispute. Indeed, if one tries to define the concepts of multipolarity and homogeneity more rigorously and precisely than I believe they can usefully be defined, it is certainly possible to argue, as George Liska has argued for instance, that "eighteenth-century Europe did not constitute a homogeneous system,"[2] and that its multipolarity was superficial in the context of the larger epochal bipolar struggle between two distinctly different worlds on either side of the Channel. In other words, depending on one's interest and perspective, one could very well understand the history of eighteenth-century European relations as one of fateful and almost heroic struggle for hegemony between two ideologically heterogeneous powers, a struggle between the French-continental world and the English-island world, separated from each other by different legal, political, and commercial systems and cultural and philosophical traditions.

Such a view, however, is possible only if one's perspective is limited to European history alone and to the period in question at that. The argument of cultural and ideologic homogeneity derives not so much from neglect of differences between the English and French or the French and Russian societies as from a comparison of the eighteenth century with other periods during which heterogeneity among European states was far more pronounced and therefore presumably more significant. Such was the case in the periods that both preceded and followed the eighteenth century. Not only were the wars of religion more violent than those fought during the period in question, but the motives behind them were far more ideological than can be said of the wars of the eighteenth century. Furthermore, as historian Gulick has demonstrated most effectively, the homogeneity of European states was not only a fact, but a fact of which European writers and statesmen were very conscious.[3] It was this consciousness of ideological homogeneity that was to become one of the first victims of the French Revolution which, as we shall show, compelled conservatives as well as revolutionaries to become acutely conscious of their ideological opposition and conflict. In retrospect, then, eighteenth-century European relations enjoyed one great advantage over those preceding and following, namely, the advantage of legitimacy and ideological consensus among independent sovereign states.

Legitimacy was of course to be found in the principle of the dynastic state, which won its formal recognition as a source of political authority and civic loyalty in the Treaty of Westphalia. The failure of the Counter Reformation to restore the lost unity of Christendom meant that the territorial division of Europe into separate sovereign states not only was an irrevocable historical fact but was legitimate as well.[4] There would no longer be any serious question of unifying all of Europe under one single authority. The territorial state became an established fact, and the map of Europe that emerged at the end of the Thirty Years' War was to remain essentially the same henceforth: divided into multiple centers of autonomous power. Multipolarity, therefore, resulted from the same historical forces as ideological homgeneity, and would remain along with it one of the most critical features of international life during the period up to the French Revolution.

The emergence of the territorial state had two seemingly contradictory results. On the one hand, new international relations could be equated with the "state of war" insofar as the rise of a state system meant open renunciation of a universal authority, even at its symbolic level. It was as if Europe had returned to the state of nature, as it were. It meant, at any rate, a more intense security dilemma for the dynastic states that had emerged from the breakup of the medieval empire. On the other hand, it must also be noted that the return to the state of nature did not exactly result in greater violence and disorder, as one might have thought would be the case. On the contrary, the division of Europe into independent and "impermeable"[5] communities forced upon the rulers of such states the sobering recognition of each other's fundamental defensibility. Their mutual relations, therefore, could not but be predicated upon the territorial integrity of dynastic states as permanent entities in the new world. Instead of being accompanied by ideological cleavage and an orgy of violence, the "state of war" among new states was characterized by

sobriety, rationalism, and secular interest in tangible achievements and concrete advantages. That is why it is justifiable to
argue that international relations were "limited" in the period
following the peace of Westphalia. They were limited in the
sense that both the aims and means of foreign policies were generally restrained and moderate compared to those in a more revolutionary age.

The limitation in the means of action was due to two things.
First, obviously the level of technology did not provide the means
of unlimited and total destruction. Second, and perhaps more significant politically, limitation in the means of action was also a
result of the dynastic form of the state which imposed on statesmen
the discipline of economizing the scarce resources available to
them.

As for the technology of warfare, wars were fought by and
large with siegecraft as their main tactical basis, even though it is
true that theorists such as Guilbert tended to depreciate the art
of fortification toward the latter part of the period. Movements
were still very slow, and the supply and transportation of arms
and other necessary materials constituted a major problem. In
this connection, it is noteworthy that from his almost experimental strategy of blitzkrieg in attacking Silesia in 1740, Frederick
he Great, probably the greatest practicing strategist of prerevolutionary Europe, had moved through the defensive warfare of
the Seven Years' War of 1756–1763 eventually to a series of
"bloodless military demonstrations and promenades" in the War
of the Bavarian Succession in 1778–1779.[6] Even a brilliant conception of an offensive and decisive strategic warfare could not
be translated into reality, owing mainly to limitations in the
available material resources.

If the resources were limited because of the rather undeveloped level of technology, the rulers of Old Europe were also severely constrained in their military actions by the nature of the
states over which they presided. Despite theoretical pretensions
to the "absolute" right to rule, there was actually nothing absolute about their real exercise of power. The monarchical governments could neither tax nobility for economic contributions nor

conscript commoners for military services. The armies, therefore, had to be composed "as much as possible of the economically unproductive elements of society,"[7] a fact which widened further the gap between the combatant and civilian elements. Voluntary enrollments were of course close to nil, while foreign mercenaries served their monarchical employers on the battlefield without that inner loyalty that is the essence of the citizen army.[8] Discipline was external and mechanical, putting a great premium upon maintaining one's own troops in line during a battle as well as economizing lives that had to be bought. Under such circumstances, destruction of the enemy, although a desirable goal, was an extremely costly affair that was not to be attempted lightly for fear of sacrificing more than rewards could possibly compensate for.

Objectives, therefore, had to be defined in the light of available means. Since the physical destruction of the enemy was next to impossible as well as being extremely costly, expectation of gains even from a successful war had to be moderated by the realization that the cost might outweigh the payoff. Thus, for instance, even Frederick the Great, who had made the greatest gains through war during the eighteenth century, was moved to write that "the Ambitious should consider above all that, armaments and military discipline being much the same throughout Europe, and alliances as a rule producing an equality of force between belligerent parties, all that princes can expect from the greatest advantages at present is to acquire, by accumulation of successes, either some small city on the frontier, or some territory which will not pay interest on the expenses of the war, and whose population does not even approach the number of citizens who perished in the campaigns."[9] War aims, in other words, had to be moderate if only because the objective conditions would not allow greater gains.

In fact it was easier to have only limited aims because, in addition to the limits in material resources, the nature of contemporary ideology was quite conducive to the spirit of moderation in international relations. It is certainly an exaggeration to speak of "the internationalism of peoples and rulers" of eighteenth-century Europe,[10] but the fact remains that ever since the failure of the Counter Reformation to stem the tide of history, Europe had been lacking in any self-conscious principle of unity. Despite the common consciousness of cultural homogeneity, there existed no formula for the international unity of Europe as a whole. Ideologically, the period between the peace of Westphalia and the outbreak of the French Revolution was a curiously vacuous one. Of course this is not to deny the fact that in the realm of creative thought, in its intellectual brilliance and aesthetic refinement, the age of the *ancien régime* is equaled by few other periods. It was the age, after all, of the *philosophes* and Rousseau. Yet, despite, or rather because of, its sophistication and secular refinement in matters of taste and sensibility, there was a degree of sobriety and spontaneity in its political life which would certainly disappear with the onset of any revolutionary movement.

It seemed not to have occurred to the monarchical heads of the *anciens régimes* that there might be a principle of legitimacy other than the one supporting their own authority and power. The territorial division of Europe into sovereign and dynastic states was accepted as if it were the dictate of Nature itself. And when the rulers sought changes for the purpose of gaining tangible advantages, they did so within the given system of international relations rather than over it. They neither entertained the illusion of omnipotence nor possessed the consciousness of a universal mission. Their guiding spirit was one of materialism, and as Montesquieu had observed in his usual astute manner, the spirit of territorial acquisition "brings with it the spirit of conservation . . . and none of that of destruction."[11] The enlightened despots may have been greedy and ambitious, but precisely because of those qualities their policies lacked the tragic dimension of a romantic revolutionary who refuses to heed the prosaic equation of means and ends. In sum, it may be said of the "absolute" rulers of the *anciens régimes* that, without intending to do so, they seem to have successfully turned their vices into virtues in that their very materialistic egoism provided the necessary foundation for a more stable and sober international life and for limited stakes in the state of war.

That such indeed was the case is proved by the historical evidence itself. Wars, which were certainly not infrequent, were nevertheless restricted in that they were waged for limited objectives with limited means, and were finally settled with indecisive results that did not alter the general equilibrium of power in the international system.

The wars of Louis XIV illustrate, oddly enough, the very opposite of what they might at first be expected to demonstrate. Against glib generalizations often found in the literature of international relations, it is certainly refreshing to read that "there was nothing 'limited' about the last war of Louis XIV."[12] Historians, too, keep reminding us that the military adventures of the celebrated Sun King had unfailingly developed into generalized "world wars."[13] However, we may ask, without denying the assertions of orthodox historians, what made the wars of Louis XIV into general wars involving other states besides direct adversaries? The answer must be, first, that the Europe of the *anciens régimes* was a system of alliances and counteralliances which in itself would have ensured a tendency toward general war. Second, what is more significant, the wars of Louis XIV were still episodes, albeit violent to a degree, in the process of medieval Europe's disintegration and the rise of the modern state system. The Sun King's military adventures could possibly have been limited to the Rhineland and northern Italy if his sole ambition had been to realize France's "natural frontiers." What always brought the whole of Europe into the wars of Louis XIV was the fact that France, a modern state par excellence, was engaged in an effort to gain advantages at the expense of two obviously moribund anachronisms, the Spanish and the Holy Roman Empires.

Nothing can illustrate the rise of the modern state system more effectively than this process of disintegration and the decline in striving for territorial impossibilities. The rise of France with her expanding population and efficient administration under Colbert and Louvois demonstrated that the future belonged to territorially limited and compact states in contrast to the cumbersome and progressively undefensible empires of the past. If the wars of Louis XIV proved anything, it was that the age of imperial unity had come to an end.

To be sure, this was a lesson that had to be learned by France as well as by her victims. There is more substance to the famed deathbed repentance of Louis XIV, who is said to have concluded his life with a confession of the futility of his excessive ambitions, than cynics are willing to acknowledge. With the rise of England and with Austria's recovery, it was inevitable that France should learn that the secret of security lay in moderate aims and limited stakes. The amazing fact is that she not only learned to live with the system of balanced power but did so before it became too late. When peace came to Europe with the ending of the War of the Spanish Succession, and the Treaty of Utrecht in 1713 formalized the gains and losses of the military adventures of Louis XIV, no enemy of France regarded her as having sinned against Europe itself. The normalization of 1715 was notable for the absence of any such general "revulsion against a power regarded as the guilty aggressor as one finds in 1814, 1918 and 1945."[14] The dynastic rulers of Europe may have regarded Louis XIV as perhaps too greedy. Louis XIV as the enemy of the system, however, as Napoleon would be regarded a century later, was quite out of the question. By the same token, no one in 1715 became self-conscious about restoring the system, as Metternich was to be in 1815, for the good reason that the system had not broken down. Instead of challenging the system itself, the wars of Louis XIV were very much part of the system. The indecisive results that were forced upon France were further proof that the multipolar system of international relations was still intact. If anything, the wars to be fought later would be even less decisive than those fought at the turn of the century.

This was certainly true of the War of the Austrian Succession, which was in fact two separate wars fought simultaneously in two separate theaters. There was the dynastic and continental struggle in which Maria Theresa fought to retain the imperial dominions against the Prussia of Frederick II, who had succeeded in securing the alliance of France and Spain. In Europe proper, the War of the Austrian Succession came to an indecisive end, since no power finally succeeded in gaining hegemony. If there was any power that emerged with profit, it was Prussia. She not only succeeded in retaining possession of Silesia in the Treaty of Dresden (1745) but, more significantly, confirmed her undeniable position as one of the major actors in the European system.

It is of course possible to see the emergence of Prussia through the Austrian Succession War as an event that in the words of one historian, "permanently and irrevocably shattered the continental balance established by the Treaty of Utrecht."[15] But from the systemic perspective, it is apparent that the rise of Prussia did nothing to destroy the fundamental structure of the existing international system. On the contrary, its net impact was to strengthen the system by adding flexibility to its operation, as the number of essential actors functioning in the system increased by one additional member in the big-power club. What is really significant is that, despite these incessant wars, none of the *anciens régimes* attempted to go all the way to establish hegemony or to secure an ideal inconsistent with the existing international system. Indeed, that wars were incessant may have been a good indication that they were rather innocuous in effect.

If wars involved only limited stakes, the same was true of diplomacy as well. Since the continuity between war and diplomacy was a fact rather than a theory, as it seems to have become today, it was only natural that the states of eighteenth-century Europe should have pursued essentially the same kind of objectives through wars and peace. Diplomacy, therefore, was an instrument of preserving the given international framework instead of being a weapon for destroying it. Complicated series of alliances and counteralliances that characterized the balance-of-power politics of the classical age were essentially aimed at maintaining the equilibrium of power, which was naturally precarious, as all political balances are bound to be. Even what historians call the "Diplomatic Revolution" of the mid-eighteenth century was, in retrospect, a fundamentally conservative event of which the net result was the minimization of the disturbance to the system coming from the old pattern of alliance reversals. In other words, far from revolutionizing the international system, the change of alliance partners, which is what the historians have in mind when they write of the "Diplomatic Revolution," helped in effect to prevent the system of balanced power from being broken up as a result of a more disruptive shift in the alliance system. The multipolar structure of the international system was kept intact although historians more concerned with the story of countries with proper names may understandably be impressed by the diplomatic shift of partners.

What actually happened was that, as Prussia rose to the status of a major power in the early half of the eighteenth century, both Austria and Russia were sufficiently alarmed to form a mutual alliance in 1746. Russia sought further security in an Anglo-Russian subsidy treaty of 1755, which in turn convinced Prussia that she could not be secure without at least neutralizing English support of Russia. As for England, her major interest lay in gaining a guarantee for the defense of Hanover, for which Austria, England's "traditional" ally, was reluctant to give a firm commitment. The result of all this was the Convention of Westminster signed by Prussia and England on January 16, 1756. This alliance in turn drove France into the arms of her "permanent" rival, Austria, thus estranging herself from her "traditional" ally, Prussia.

The separation of France from Prussia was of course what Prince Kaunitz of Vienna had hoped for all along, he having initially concluded that the European balance could not be preserved without limiting Prussia's rising power by isolating her from her traditional ally, France. In achieving his immediate aim of turning France away from Berlin and toward Vienna, however, Prince Kaunitz, the supreme representative of the classical diplomacy of the eighteenth century, did not really gain any permanent net advantage. On the contrary, all the other major states acted in such a way as to minimize the gain of any single power and maximize as a consequence the stability of the balance-of-power system itself. In other words, it was quite impossible for Austria to weaken Prussia substantially, because the former's diplomatic maneuvers could always be met by appropriate countermoves by the latter. Short of a revolution, the stakes of diplomacy were, therefore, as limited as those of warfare.

However, Austria was not, of course, going to accept without a struggle Prussia's new status as one of the great powers. The Seven Years' War of 1756–1763 was a result of Austria's military preparations for such a struggle, which led Frederick the Great of Prussia to strike a preemptive blow. As in previous wars of the century, this war between Prussia and Austria was easily generalized, with France and Britain once again fighting each other on the seas and for the colonies. The result was as indecisive as in the case of previous wars. The Peace of Hubertusburg, signed on February 15, 1763, put an end to the continental war by formally acknowledging the stalemate between Prussia and Austria. The colonial war was more violent and ended with Britain more decisively victorious. But the concluding Treaty of Paris, signed on February 10, 1763, left France still a first-rate power, thanks to the astute diplomacy of the Duke of Choiseul.

Nothing, in other words, was fundamentally changed by these wars. From the perspective of the systemic structure, the chief significance of the Seven Years' War lay in having actually consolidated the positions won by Prussia and Russia in the general European balance of power. The number of essential actors in the system had now permanently increased to five, making the operation of the balance-of-power system even more flexible than before. In fact, international relations on the eve of the French Revolution seemed to have hardened most successfully into a multipolar, homogeneous system, after having gone through a series of conflicts, both military and diplomatic. The end result of the conflicts had been to demonstrate that no permanent structural changes would be effected to alter the fundamental equilibrium of power unless an event of revolutionary proportion were to occur. Such an event was the French Revolution.

In the meantime, however, interstate relations were characterized by limited warfare, moderation in diplomatic aims, and general stability of the basic equilibrium of power. In other words, the system of international relations under the *ancien régime* was stable on two accounts. First, it was guaranteed, as long as it remained homogeneous and multipolar, against a total and unrestrained struggle for hegemony. Its competitions and rivalries were limited not only because the available means of destruction would not allow more violent and decisive engagements, but more significantly because they resembled what game theorists call variable-sum games in that there was no consciousness of one overriding principle of unity to be imposed upon the entire European world. It was a curiously cynical and unromantic age. Struggles were directed toward concrete advantages and tangible benefits rather than matters of spiritual dimension. Royal heads of states were in all probability as Machiavellian as political rulers of any other age, but perhaps because of their cynicism and materialism they escaped, it seems in retrospect, one fatal quality that characterizes all revolutionaries and total struggles: the spiritual egoism of believing in a selfless ideal. The result of this secular sobriety that prevailed among the rulers of the *ancien régime* was that for the most part each took the others' survival for granted. The system, to put it another way, was stable because its members were virtually guaranteed against destruction unto death.

Having said that, however, it must immediately be called to attention that such an optimistic characterization of eighteenth-century Europe omits one significant aspect of the period. If there was security for the major states—or essential actors—of the system, the same cannot as certainly be said of those states that had only a marginal status in the entire balance-of-power system. For the latter, the system was a cruel environment in which to survive. The very cynicism that saved the major states from a total and unrestrained war also tended to turn small and marginal states into helpless prey for the dominant ones. The fate of Poland, which was carved up again and again for the nourishment of more powerful neighbors, is of course the most glaring example of the sort of prejudice against small states that was inherent in the multipolar system itself. We can also cite the examples of the Ottoman Empire, Sweden, and Silesia, all of which came under the system of territorial compensations and readjustments so characteristic of the oligopolistic competition in the classical balance-of-power system. Indeed, the entire colonial struggle between the British and the French in North America, India, and the Caribbean was a glaring instance of the almost clinical detachment that the major states of eighteenth-century Europe felt for the interests of those who had the misfortune not to be born in one of their own domains.

From a systemic perspective, however, the callous disregard for the interest and integrity of small states in the classical balance-of-power system may well have been one of the functional requirements for the maintenance of the system. As Stanley Hoffmann put it, it could be that there was need for "a frontier zone where the major states can expand without fatally colliding, which is a prerequisite of the kind of flexibility that a balancing system needs."[16] In other words, what saved the major powers from an unrestrained zero-sum struggle was probably not their ideological homogeneity as such nor even the reality of multiple centers of autonomous and equivalent power. In the final analysis it may have to be argued that they were kept from coming to fatal blows against each other because they were able to direct their blows against helpless, small, and often non-European states. If this analysis is correct, it would suggest a kind of "new-frontier" theory of international stability, and furthermore it may invite greater effort in the psychological study of aggressive drives.

It certainly does not seem that such a new-frontier thesis would by itself negate the role of ideological factors in international relations. On the contrary, even if such a theory were empirically validated, the historical evidence would still suggest that the factor of ideological homogeneity was quite crucial to the question of international stability. Witness the impact of the French Revolution. It is hard to imagine that the situation had materially changed with regard to the place of small states and colonial areas during the period in which the stability of the classical balance-of-power system had given way to the struggle of revolutionary and Napoleonic wars. The critical factor here must have been the rise of an ideologically dissimilar state with increasingly revolutionary ambitions, and its effect upon the international relations of the *ancien régime*. In this sense, I believe it is legitimate to limit our analysis to the impact of the French Revolution as such, recognizing of course that such an analysis will give us not a complete but only a partial picture of the entire process of international destabilization.

What is then involved in the concept of international destabilization? Or to put the question more concretely, what do we mean when we assert that the stability of the classical international system of the *ancien régime* had broken down during the period of the French Revolution and the Napoleonic Empire? At the minimum, the breakdown of international stability or any other kind of stability in a social system implies a sudden disappearance of the routine or typical pattern of behavior that is the essence of a stable relationship. It means, first, the loss of basic agreement about the rules of the game, and, second, the appearance of forms of action that are in conflict with the established norms of the social system. The breakdown of international stability, therefore, does not necessarily mean permanent and irrevocable destruction of the existing international system. Indeed, novel forms of action do often manage to become in time integral parts of the routine which constitutes the basis of stability. Therefore, the critical issue is not whether the breakdown of international stability during the French Revolution constituted a permanent historical transformation, although I myself happen to believe that the changes in the nature of interstate relations that resulted from the Revolution and other related political upheavals were of an irreversible and secular kind. What is more important for our purpose is that, apart from the question of historical transformation, the impact of the Revolution was such as to have substantially damaged the limited nature of classical international relations to the extent of removing in effect those limits that were essential to the balance-of-power system of the eighteenth century. To borrow Stanley Hoffmann's expression again, the French Revolution had done no less than change "the stakes of conflict," thereby destroying the competitive but civilized life among the dynastic rulers of the major states.

In sum, the international relations of the revolutionary age exhibited the following characteristics.

1. *Total aims:* The struggle for unlimited hegemony was

once again the essence of international politics. Whether reluctantly or deliberately, all the major European powers would be involved in the struggle unto death, which could not be brought to an end except through either total destruction or political transformation of one side or the other. Transformation—that is, the restoration of monarchy in France—was the result. In the meantime, the objectives of foreign policies were no longer limited to advantages to be gained within the given framework of multipolar equilibrium. The important question became one of mastery versus survival—and when the outcomes are so starkly antithetical, the international system will in all probability be at its lowest point in the scale of stability.

2. *Total means:* Total aims do not automatically destroy international stability. For the latter to become reality, far more effective means of destruction than those that had been available in the past were needed—and they did become available. The switch from the use of hired mercenary troops to the creation of the citizen army had unprecedented revolutionary consequences, which even those who created the citizen army had scarcely anticipated. The accelerating use of fire power for decisive battles was further to add to the already escalating range and degree of violence. The struggle for hegemony was no longer theoretical, as Frederick the Great had assumed it would be. It was rapidly becoming reality.

3. *Unlimited stakes:* Total aims plus total means naturally produced unlimited stakes of the conflict. It was no longer a question of what the states wanted but what they could not avoid struggling for. The probable outcomes of their conflicts were such as to affect their very survival, not only because they or some among them consciously wanted to destroy one another, but also because the means of achieving such a purpose were becoming increasingly available. The traditional ceiling on the stakes of conflict was fast disappearing. Penalty for defeat was no longer an unfavorable but indecisive territorial rearrangement. At stake was the very principle of legitimacy itself and with it the continued existence of the established forms of international life.

With the benefit of hindsight, it is quite clear that these changes in the aims, means, and stakes of international relations were closely related to the systemic change or, more specifically, the changes in the systemic environment. Although the aims and means belong essentially to the subsystemic level of analysis, as they are related to foreign policies of states, the changes at the systemic level were no less pronounced. These were of course the changes in the ideological situation and the configuration of forces. As for the former, the repudiation of royalism and the dynastic principle of legitimacy in revolutionary France had injected a radically heterogeneous element into the hitherto homogeneous European society of dynastic states and royal rulers. For the latter, the sudden demonstration of France's potential power and revolutionary ambition had eventually compelled conservative states of Europe into an anti-French coalition, thereby transforming the multipolar structure of the international system into a virtually bipolar one. The important question then is: How were these two systemic changes related to the changes in the stakes of conflict itself?

In the first place, it is clear that the bipolarization was a product of ideological revolution, although the power potential of France in the form of her population, geography, and social development was there to begin with. It is therefore essentially correct to assert that what destroyed the stability of prerevolutionary international relations was the new ideological element. But to assert that really does not explain anything, except to suggest a problem. It does not explain anything because, given the proposition that ideological heterogeneity led to the breakdown of international stability, we still need to know precisely how and why this was the case. To be sure, one might take the position, which I myself regard as banal and rather trivial, that ideology means a set of aims and values and therefore a major state with a revolutionary ideology is bound to pursue international goals antithetical to the *status quo*. Such a view, it seems to me, derives basically from our own contemporary experiences with Nazism and later the Cold War. Even here it is quite apparent that such a simplistic view of the role of ideological factors in international politics is at best no more than a suggestion of a problem to be explored. Quite often it is really a devil theory of history which is often found in the crude imagination of the popular mind. What we ought to do, it should be clear by now, is to take the link between the role of ideology and the breakdown of international stability as a problem to be solved and then try to solve it through a careful and detached analysis of actual historical situations and processes. The object of such a study is to define more unambiguously than has been possible so far the nature of the impact of ideological heterogeneity on international stability and lay bare the processes of interaction between the systemic environment and individual actions of component states. This is precisely what this study hopes to accomplish in the following pages.

Notes

1. Leopold Ranke, "The Great Powers," translated by Theodore H. von Laue and included in his *Leopold Ranke: The Formative Years* (Princeton, 1950), p. 189.
2. George Liska, "Continuity and Change in International Systems," *World Politics,* Vol. XVI (Oct., 1963), p. 121.
3. Edward Vose Gulick, *Europe's Classical Balance of Power, A Case History of the Theory and Practice of One of the Great Concepts of European Statecraft* (New York, 1967), pp. 19–24.
4. On the evolution of legal thought concerning the nature of state and war, see Walter Schiffer, *The Legal Community of Mankind* (New York, 1954), Chaps. 2 and 3.
5. On the concept of "impermeable" state, see John H. Herz, *International Politics in the Atomic Age* (New York, 1959), pp. 43–61.
6. E. M. Earle, ed., *Makers of Modern Strategy, Military Thought from Machiavelli to Hitler* (Princeton, 1943), p. 65.
7. *Ibid.,* p. 58.
8. The idea of a citizen army was a common theme among such writers as Montesquieu, Rousseau, and others. Guilbert, who, as a military thinker, gave perhaps the most succinct expression by suggesting the citizen army as the means for a war of movement instead of a war of position, was nevertheless resigned for all practical purposes to the reality of the hired soldiers. Like Frederick the Great before him, Guilbert was convinced that the citizen army was an unattainable dream. See the excellent discussion by R. R. Palmer, in E. M. Earle, *op. cit.,* pp. 63–64.
9. Frederick II, in *Politisches Testament von 1752,* quoted by R. R. Palmer, in E. H. Earle, *op. cit.,* p. 61.
10. Richard Rosecrance, *Action and Reaction in World Politics, International Systems in Perspective* (Boston, 1963), p. 20.
11. Montesquieu, *L'Esprit des lois,* I, 3, quoted by Albert Sorel,

L'Europe et la Révolution française, 8 vols., 9th ed. (Paris, 1905), Vol. I, pp. 332–333.

12. George Liska, *op. cit.,* p. 122.

13. John B. Wolf, *The Emergence of the Great Powers, 1685–1715* (New York, 1951), Chap. II. See also Penfield Roberts, *The Quest for Security, 1715–1740* (New York, 1947), p. 1.

14. Penfield Roberts, *op. cit.,* p. 242.

15. Walter L. Dorn, *Competition for Empire, 1740–1763* (New York, 1940), p. 122.

16. Stanley Hoffman, *The State of War, Essays in the Theory and Practice of International Politics* (New York, 1965), p. 95.

17. *Ibid.,* p. 92.

II

The Origins of the War:
The Role of Ideology in Perception and Communication

The Revolution destroyed the classical balance-of-power system. But it is not certain that the destruction of the classical balance-of-power system was inevitable. In fact, the course of the Revolution itself was always partly contingent and accidental as much as it was "necessary" and predictable. After all, the gap between the Revolution of 1789 and the Terror of 1793 is a very real one—and it does no good to insist on the continuity of the revolutionary process, if the very real differences between one stage of the Revolution and another are not properly taken into account.

By the same token, it is misleading to see the impact of the Revolution on the interstate relations of the time only in terms of its final and destructive effect. This is more apparent to later historians with the benefit of hindsight than it was to contemporaries. To be sure, it may be a profound insight to see the system-destructive impact of the Revolution as deeply rooted in the nature of the Revolution itself. It is utterly unrewarding, however, to conclude from this that the effect of the Revolution on European interstate relations was equally destructive from the beginning to the end. On the contrary, there was very little in the early stage of the Revolution which would have made the dissolution of the classical balance-of-power system "inevitable" without later developments in the course of the Revolution itself. The relations be-

tween revolutionary France and the rest of Europe were far from
being ideological at the outset. It was only at the later stage of the
Revolution that the struggle became one of ideological confrontation. At first, neither France nor Europe entertained any grand
ideological designs on each other. Their antagonisms were quite
traditional, rooted in rivalries and jealousies of long standing.

What, then, transformed these relatively stable tensions into
an unpredictable kind of ideological struggle? The first violent
contact came in 1792, when revolutionary France declared war on
April 20 against the "House of Austria," a war that would eventually engulf the whole of Europe and Britain in an unforeseen
struggle for survival—and "legitimacy." It would become an ideological war. But in 1792, despite the Burkian rhetoric, neither the
revolutionaries nor the conservatives interpreted their interests in
ideological terms.

As a matter of fact, Europe's reaction to the French Revolution had been primarily intellectual rather than political. Everywhere in Europe, from Belfast to St. Petersburg, it was mainly men
of thought and letters who were stirred by the great upheavals now
taking place in Paris. With a few notable exceptions, the storming
of the Bastille was met with approval and enthusiasm by both
masses and publicists. In Germany, although Goethe and Schiller
seem to have hesitated, other illustrious figures, such as Kant,
Fichte, Herder, Johannes von Müller, and even young Hegel,
supported the Revolution, while in England even the ruling
classes did not disapprove of what they believed to be French efforts to emulate the British in a constitutional government. On
the whole, the crowned rulers of European states were either in-
different or kept prudently silent, with the exception of the rather
inconsequential Gustavus III of Sweden, who was very anxious to
lead a crusade against the Revolution. Such successful men of routine as Pitt of England and Leopold of Austria were not easily
persuaded by ideological arguments. To them, the Revolution in
Paris meant no more than bad luck for the French Bourbons who
were now incapacitated, in their smug conservative view, from
playing an active role in the game of European politics. France,
for the moment, had to be counted out of the game. As for the

game itself, there was no doubt in their minds that it would go on as usual.

Of course the game was not to continue as usual. After all, the National Assembly of France had already announced in the summer of 1789 an end to "the feudal regime."[1] The implications of such a declaration might have been limited to the domestic scene had it not been for the fact that the French Bourbons had claimed sovereignty over the province of Alsace on the basis of the Treaty of Münster.[2] Alsace, however, was under several German princes who enjoyed feudal, hence more substantial, rights over the domain and were now naturally alarmed by France's public disavowal of all feudal rights and obligations. It is tempting at this point to see this conflict over the validity of feudal rights as the primary cause of ideological war, since such an explanation would be so "consistent" with the later development of relations between revolutionary France and conservative Europe.

Reality, however, was more complicated. In the first place, it was not the first time that a conflict had arisen over the Alsatian domain. In obviously nonrevolutionary contexts, the German princes had previously protested against France's violation of what they were convinced were their rights.[3] The Alsatian issue was essentially a conflict of rights and not necessarily a conflict of values.

In fact, the French were quite prepared to negotiate over the territorial dispute. Despite the exaggerated rhetoric of some of its more extremist members, the National Assembly, at the initiative of its Diplomatic Committee, decided to negotiate indemnities for the affected princes of the Holy Roman Empire. Mirabeau, who directed the Diplomatic Committee, was convinced that a failure to find a diplomatic solution for the feudal enclave problem would lead to war, and he succeeded in persuading Montmorin, Minister of Foreign Affairs, to make several attempts to negotiate with the German princes. France's diplomatic initiatives, however, were met with an adamant demand by the aggrieved princes for the restoration of their rights. They would have nothing to do with indemnities. Perhaps interpreting France's willingness to negotiate as a sign of her weakness, the princes appealed to the

Diet of the Empire for a decisive action against France, possibly involving military intervention.[4]

But the imperial Diet was not easily moved. Only Prussia seemed to find the idea of acting against France appealing, since a conflict between Austria and her "traditional ally," France, would naturally benefit, according to the logic of the classical balance-of-power system, only their common competitor, namely Prussia. For precisely the same reason, Austria was bound to resist any pressure to involve herself in a conflict that would tip the balance in favor of Prussia, her "traditional" enemy. Whatever ideological implications the feudal-rights problem might have had, Leopold was more concerned with the maintenance of the *status quo,* which, in his view, was not apparently threatened by France's domestic upheavals. Without the Emperor's approval the Diet was helpless to act.

The Empire, however, was under greater pressure from another source, namely members of the French nobility who had emigrated from France since 1789. Most of them had settled in the Rhineland and were now exerting themselves in a reactionary crusade against the Revolution in France. Their first objective, since there was no question of their being able to act alone, despite pretensions to military preparations,[5] was to move the Empire against France. For this purpose they were engaged in what might be described as the politics of lobbying, trying to persuade not only the Emperor himself but the various princes of Germany by appealing to their interests as well as their supposed ideals.

All this was to no avail. As Leopold wrote to his sister, Marie-Antoinette, as late as January 31 in 1792, less than three months before France would declare war against Austria, he was convinced that "the restoration of the old regime [in France] would be an impossible thing to accomplish."[6] As an authentic conservative, he was reconciled to what seemed to him to be an already accomplished fact in France. After all, did not Louis XVI himself accept the Constitution of 1791? Leopold had already turned down a request by Sweden's King, Gustavus III, for the use of the port of Ostend in a military crusade against the wicked Jacobins in Paris.[7] He was not now likely to be moved by the pleadings of lesser figures than Gustavus III.

The *émigrés'* intrigues, however, produced at least one tangible result, the crucial Pillnitz declaration of August 1791 in which two "traditional enemies," the Emperor and the King of the Hohenzollerns, were brought together to express a common concern with the predicament of the French Bourbons. It was of course not the *émigrés* alone who had contributed to the making of the declaration. The repeated appeals of the French royal family, the fiasco of Varennes, the warnings of conservative ideologists, and the "German" convictions of such new men as Bischoffswerder in Prussia and Cobenzle and Spielmann in Austria—all of these undoubtedly put great pressure on the Emperor to do something.[8]

The declaration itself was harmless enough. It merely announced that the German powers were prepared to intervene in French affairs to protect the French Bourbons "if" the powers of Europe agreed to act jointly on the matter. As Leopold himself was well aware, the chances of the European powers coming together in a joint action were very slim. The often-quoted "if" clause (*"alors et dans ce cas"*) should have ensured that the declaration of Pillnitz would not be taken too seriously. Indeed the astute sister of the Emperor confessed to seeing in the declaration little assurance of "foreign help."[9]

The effect of the declaration on the French, however, was a different matter. It at once strengthened the arguments of those who wanted a war. Led by Jacques Pierre Brissot, the leading light of a group known later as Girondins, who immediately responded to the Pillnitz declaration by advocating a direct attack on the Rhineland, most of those who wanted a foreign war, whatever their real motivations, now found a perfect justification for their stand. If the Brissotins were primarily concerned to expose traitors to the Revolution by forcing them to make their stand clear under exigencies of a foreign military action, those on the extreme right were convinced that a decisive military action by the European powers would easily topple the revolutionary government and return France to its rightful owners. Only Robespierre and a few others maintained their position against a rising cry for war. Convinced that the first task of the Revolution was to consolidate its achievements within France, Robespierre, much like Stalin in our century, argued for "democracy in one country," as it were.[10] The tide, however, was turning against Robespierre. Even the moderates, the so-called "Feuillants," were being won over by the prowar argument. Danton, the opportunist, did not fail to notice the turn of the popular sentiment, and by December 17, 1791 he had completely changed his position to side with the prowar party.[11]

As for the German powers, they were not exactly helping the antiwar party. Mainly thanks to the work of men like Bischoffswerder, Cobenzle and Spielmann, who were not orthodox in the same sense that Kaunitz and Hertzberg were, the Emperor and the Prussian King were again brought together in a treaty establishing the Austro-Prussian alliance of February 7, 1792, through which they arranged for common defense and announced their intentions to pursue a concert of powers to regulate French affairs. Despite the ominous language of the treaty, it is not likely that Leopold really intended to act in concert with Prussia against France—but his days were numbered. The Emperor, who had consistently kept a check on the more active elements, died suddenly on March 1, to be succeeded by Francis II, a young man more easily given to adventures.

The stage was now set for the final drift into war. If Germany was seemingly united against revolutionary France, the antiwar parties within France itself were being literally shouted down by the Girondists, who had by late January of 1792 shifted the main object of their attack from the *émigrés* to Louis XVI himself. After all, had not the King and his Austrian Queen tried already to flee from France, possibly to join forces with and take charge of a counterrevolution? When the King, insulted by the Girondin rhetoric, had retaliated by dismissing Narvonne, the darling of the war party, from the ministry of war, the Girondists, who controlled the Diplomatic Committee of the Assembly, retorted by forcing the King to fire the moderate de Lessart from the ministry of foreign affairs.[12] De Lessart, who had done much to keep the crisis from reaching the boiling point, was to perish later in the prison guarded by the Jacobins.

Within a week after the dismissal of de Lessart on March 10, the King was forced to entrust the entire cabinet to a new set of men, whose political leanings were unreservedly Jacobin. The ministry of foreign affairs went to a man who is supposed to have told de Lessart that "you will not only have a war with Austria, but a general European war." Charles Fronçois Duperrier, better known as Dumouriez, also added, not without his share of cynicism, that "it shall . . . only end in bringing us glory, profit, and extended dominion."[13] As Minister of Foreign Affairs, he was now to translate his assumptions into reality.

One of his more tenuous assumptions was that in the event of a war between France and Austria, England and Prussia would remain at least "neutral," a conviction which led him to do everything to provoke the Assembly into declaring a war against Austria. After a predictable series of communications, or more correctly miscommunications, between Vienna and Paris, which were becoming more threatening with every new note, Dumouriez announced to the Assembly on April 20 that the latest statement from Vienna amounted to "a virtual declaration of war."[14] Without any delay, the Assembly passed a proposal, put forward personally by Louis XVI who was obviously under duress, for a declaration of war against the King of Bohemia and Hungary, that is, against Austria but not the Empire. The King put his signature to the declaration that afternoon, thus opening a new fateful chapter in the history of Europe. Not unexpectedly, Condorcet provided the justification. The French nation, according to his speech of April 20, had no intention of making any territorial conquest. The only reason for taking up arms was to defend its freedom from the unjust attack of a foreign king.[15] Historians would differ.

●   ●   ●

Two eminent historians on the subject, Heinrich von Sybel and Albert Sorel, have both blamed the Girondin politicians for causing an unnecessary war. As if to validate the well-known thesis of Karl Mannheim, both historians seem to have had certain political reasons for singling out the Girondin "party"[16] for war guilt. To the German historian, it was obviously more satisfactory to blame the French, while Sorel equated the Girondins with democratic politics for which he had little sympathy. In the absence of any ideological interest in the Mannheimian sense, I find such apportionment of war guilt rather trivial.

The Girondin rhetoric, which knew no sense of limits, makes it very easy to regard the war of 1792 as *guerre universelle* brought about by the ideological excesses of the muddle-headed Jacobins. After all, it was Brissot and his cohorts who had led the Legislative Assembly into declaring "the just defense of a free people against the unjust aggression of a King."[17] A more interesting question—more interesting from a sociological if not a moral point of view—concerns "how" and "why" rather than "who." If the Girondin politicians led by Brissot had actually brought about war between revolutionary France and conservative Europe, we cannot surely be satisfied with a mere moral reproach for their excesses. We must ask: How was it that the Girondists were able to bring France into war?

This is no idle question when we consider the following facts. In the first place, the Legislative Assembly was not originally in favor of war. There were only 136 members who could be identified as Jacobins out of the total of 745. Aside from 264 Feuillants, the remaining 345 members were uncommitted independents. Even among the Jacobins, there was an active minority opposed to a foreign war at that time. Robespierre is the most illustrious name in this group, but even Danton, along with a few other influential figures, was opposed to Brissot's ideas at the beginning. There were also a few influential newspapers supporting Robespierre on the question of war.[18] Why was it, then, that the voice of Robespierre and others who supported him were drowned out later in the rising chorus of the war party?

The fact is that the war of 1792 was a product of circumstances beyond the control of any individual. It is of course dangerous to impute "necessity" to history. But even riskier would it be to see the actions of a few individuals out of the social context in which they operated. The Girondists succeeded in their aim of inciting France to a war against Austria because the situation both in and out of France was ripe for their more radical program of action. Robespierre could not stem the tide in 1792 because both the domestic political situation in France and the pattern of relations between revolutionary France and conservative Europe favored the irresponsible demagogy of such men as Brissot, Dumas, Vergniaud, Isnard, Condorcet, and Hérault de Sechelles. Danton knew better whither the tide was turning.[19]

On the domestic side, two factors contributed to the success of the war party. In the first place, there was what might loosely be called the popular revolutionary imagination, which was a product of fear as well as hope. With the benefit of hindsight, it is of course easy to dismiss the threat of counterrevolution as not serious, but to the contemporaries it was a different story. Surrounded by the hostile crowns, the men of 1789 could not afford to take the survival of the Revolution for granted. The quest for security naturally became obsessive, turning into a defiant assertion of a messianic zeal which in essence was deeply rooted in the sense of insecurity itself. The Constituent Assembly's renunciation of all wars of conquest in May of 1790 necessarily had two sides, one the implication that other conservative powers were perfectly willing to wage wars of conquest, and the other the universalism of the revolutionary spirit, as found later in such an almost Sartrian statement as "You embrace the cause of other peoples in embracing your own."[20] What was lacking in the revolutionary imagination was an appreciation of the concrete and a confidence in relative security.

In the second place, to make matters worse, the attempted flight of Louis XVI had only confirmed the popular suspicion of the King's ultimate loyalty. The crisis thus brought about by the fiasco of Varennes resulted in the strengthening of those who had argued all along that there was a concerted effort on the part of European monarchs to crush the Revolution and undo its achievements. The revolutionary imagination had at last found a tangible vindication of its own diagnosis of the reality. The process of transforming a timid fear of counterrevolution into a determination to defend the Revolution against the reaction was now complete and irreversible.

On the international side, the outstanding fact was the breakdown of meaningful communication. Particularly when the flight to Varennes was followed by the Pillnitz declaration, there seemed to be no longer any possibility of a meaningful dialogue between Paris and Vienna. Dispatches from Vienna would be viewed in Paris stripped of their subtler implications and polite evasions, while the conservative statesmen in Vienna, or for that matter in Berlin and London as well, would persist in looking through their own glasses darkly. Reflecting on the pattern of miscommunication, as it were, between revolutionary France and conservative Europe, one is tempted to apply Richard Snyder's decision-making analysis, which relies heavily on the decision-makers' perception of reality rather than "reality" itself.[21] We do not, however, have to use the elaborate scheme proposed by Professor Snyder in its formal sense. Even without putting our material into "boxes" as suggested by the formal model, the conclusion is quite obvious that the most conspicuous feature of international relations on the eve of the 1792 war was the gap between reality and the actors' perceptions of reality. Actually, no counterrevolutionary crusade was imminent, although, on the other hand, the progressive democratization of revolutionary France posed a serious threat to the stability of international relations throughout Europe. In retrospect, it is the statesmen of Vienna and London who should have been alarmed at the implications of the Revolution. In actual fact it was the revolutionaries who were convinced that Europe was about to undo the accomplishments of 1789.

The gap between perception and reality was of course chiefly due to the conceptual schemes within which the main actors operated. If the conservatives, except those who were either by profession or temperament devoted to "ideological thinking," interpreted the domestic upheavals of France within the familiar framework of their own traditional experience, the revolutionaries, on the other hand, tended to project their own universalistic tendencies on the conservatives. The result was inevitably a breakdown in international communications—and with it, the breakdown of stability in international relations. This in sum is the pattern of interaction between the Revolution and Europe that led to war.

It would be wrong, however, to conclude that the war was ideological in the sense that the belligerents pursued ideological aims from the outset. They did not pursue ideological aims.[22] In 1792, there existed no grand design to restore the old regime in France. Nor was it really the purpose of the French to revolutionize other countries by the war. If the conservative statesmen were naturally cynical and materialistic, the Girondin politicians too were not free from their share of petty political interests, as their involvement in the commercial interests of the Bordeaux merchants proves. Dumouriez, as pointed out earlier, fancied himself as a realist who was now to launch an adventure intended to benefit France territorially and financially.

The aims, to be sure, would become ideological, but in terms of its origins, the war of 1792 was ideological only in a different sense—that it was a product of what may loosely be called a revolutionary situation. It was born of pressures deriving from the domestic crisis in France on the one hand and the breakdown of international communications on the other, the second being obviously a result of the first.

In more general terms, the analysis of the causes of the war of 1792 may lead us to the following observation. In the first place, the most immediate and critical impact of the Revolution was to transform the political structure of France in such a way as to thrust the power of foreign-policy-making upon those whose perception of interstate relations was radically different from that of traditional rulers. It was not so much that the new men in France wanted to disobey the rules of the old game. As evidenced by the unexpected reception of the Pillnitz declaration, their main trouble was that they were not familiar with matters that could be routine to the men of the old world. The radically different structure that they perceived practically guaranteed international misunderstandings and miscalculations. It was almost inevitable, therefore, that the international system now composed of heterogeneous units would suffer from a progressively malfunctioning communications process.

In the second place, if the critical role of France was to transform the international system from a homogeneous to a heterogeneous one, conservative powers further aggravated the disruptive tendencies in the system by failing to recognize the fact that the political transformation in France had produced an international actor with a new perceptual scheme. Had they realized this, it is possible either that they would have attempted to liquidate the French Revolution and restore the ancient regime, as Burke was advocating, or else would not have committed such a blunder as issuing a declaration which could not but be misconstrued by the revolutionaries. The fact was that the crowned rulers were all securely attached to the familiar, and failing to see the novelty of 1789, did not hesitate to act within the framework of the classical interstate system. If it would not offend the literary sensibilities of historians proper, it might even be said here that the war of 1792 was a product of the lack of an adequate adaptive mechanism in the traditional balance-of-power system—a mechanism that could have enabled the system to survive the shock of the Revolution without being dissolved as it actually was. Such a mechanism was completely absent, since the last thing the crowned rulers felt they had reason to dread was any threat to international stability that might be posed by a state in the throes of revolutionary distress. In their innocent confidence in the permanence of life as they had known it, they did not believe that the Revolution in France injected a completely new element into international politics. Between revolutionary France and conservative Europe, the lack of understanding was quite mutual—and mutually reenforcing as well.

Finally, despite the fact that its origins were deeply rooted in the nature of the Revolution and the international system, one should not exaggerate the importance of the war at this point. This war was not an ideological struggle yet, and the dissolution of the classical balance-of-power system was neither complete nor absolutely assured. To see how the war in fact came to spell the destruction of the international system, we have to turn to its later development.

Notes

1. J. Mavidal, E. Laurent, *et al.*, eds., *Archives parlementaires, recueil complet des débats législatifs et politiques, des Chambres françaises de 1789 à 1860*, Ser. I (Paris, 1868–1870), Vol. VIII, pp. 397–398. Hereafter referred to as *Archives parlementaires*.

2. The relevant article in the Treaty is 89. See H. Vast, ed., *Les Grands Traités du Régime de Louis XIV* (Paris, 1839, 1899), Vol. I, pp. 38–39. Consult also P. Muret, "L'affaire des princes possessiones d'Alsace et les origines du conflit entre la Révolution et l'Europe," *Revue d'histoire moderne et contemporaine* (Paris, 1899–1900), Vol. I, p. 433.

3. Sidney S. Biro, *The German Policy of Revolutionary France; A Study in French Diplomacy During the War of the First Coalition, 1792–1797* (Cambridge, Mass., 1957), Vol. I, pp. 39–40.

4. Sagnac, *Le Rhin française pendant le Révolution et l'Empire* (Paris, 1917), pp. 55 ff.

5. See Monthly Report of I. von Hertwich, Office-Director of the Imperial Embassy at Coblenz, end of 1791, as quoted by S. S. Biro, *op. cit.*, Vol. I, p. 43.

6. A. R. von Arneth, ed., *Marie-Antoinette, Joseph II und Leopold II: Ihr Briefwechsel* (Leipzig, 1866), p. 282.

7. Count Axel Fersen, *Diary and Correspondence of Count Axel Fersen, Grand-Marshal of Sweden, Relating to the Court of France*, translated by K. P. Wormeley (Boston, 1902), pp. 124 ff.

8. See Heinrich von Sybel, *History of the French Revolution*, translated by Walter C. Perry, 4 vols. (London, 1867–1869), Vol. II, pp. 6–11.

9. Marie-Antoinette to Count Fersen, Sept. 26, 1791, in Fersen, *op. cit.*, p. 165.

10. On the positions of Robespierre and Brissot, see G. Walter, *Robespierre* (Paris, 1946), pp. 231–241.

11. Albert Mathiez, *Danton et la paix* (Paris, 1919), pp. 6–12.

12. *Reimpression de l'ancien Moniteur* (Paris, 1858–1870), Vol. XI, pp. 597–608. Hereafter referred to as *Moniteur*. The Assembly's action was in violation of the Constitution of 1791, which made the ministers responsible only to the King and not to the Assembly.

13. Quoted by Heinrich von Sybel, *op. cit.*, Vol. I, p. 441.

14. J. Hansen, ed., *Quellen zur Geschichte des Rheinlandes in Zeitalter der französischen Revolution, 1780–1801* (Bonn, 1931–1938), Vol. II, p. 99.

15. *Moniteur*, Vol. XII, pp. 186–188.

16. A recent study of the Girondin denies the existence of the Girondin "party." See M. J. Sydenham, *The Girondin* (London, 1961). For the purposes of the present study, however, it does not seem inappropriate to regard Brissot and a group of deputies who were associated with him as constituting at least a faction, if not a party. After all, the Brissotins took a recognizable lead in pressing for war in 1792.

17. *Moniteur*, Vol. XII, pp. 182–188, contains the text of the French declaration of war.

18. See Georges Lefebvre, *The French Revolution from Its Origins to 1793*, translated by E. M. Evanson (New York, 1962), p. 218.

19. A. Fribourg, ed., *Discours de Danton* (Paris, 1910), pp. 121–123. See also A. Mathiez, *Danton et la paix* (Paris, 1919), pp. 6–12.

20. Condorcet, as reported in *Révolutions de Paris,* Vol. XI, No. 9 (Jan. 7, 1792), p. 12 quoted by Crane Brinton in *A Decade of Revolution, 1789–1799* (New York, 1934), p. 56.

21. Richard C. Snyder, H. W. Bruck, and Burton Sapin, *Foreign Policy Decision-Making, An Approach to the Study of International Politics* (New York, 1962).

22. R. R. Palmer, *The Age of the Democratic Revolution: A Political History of Europe and America, 1760–1800,* Vol. I: *The Struggle* (Princeton, 1964), p. 14.

III

The "Second" Revolution: *The Impact of International Relations on the Domestic Political System*

In the spring of 1792, neither revolutionary France, which declared war against Austria, nor conservative German powers, which did nothing to avert the drift to a war with France, had any inkling of what was in store for them. It was simply beyond their imagination that a war so inauspiciously begun would come to involve the whole European world in bloodshed lasting a quarter of a century. Today of course it is not difficult to see that the war had actually begun in no ordinary circumstances. Indeed, for historians, the temptation is strong to see the causes for the destruction of the classical balance of power in the very circumstances in which a revolutionary power came into an open conflict with the conservative states. Such a retrospective view, however, overlooks the fact that at the outset of the war neither side was seriously proposing to impose its own ideological system upon the other. In the event of a conservative victory, certainly—which both Vienna and Berlin were convinced would be quick in coming—the crowned heads of Europe would not have hesitated to place a check on the Jacobin radicalism, but the restoration of the old regime was hardly the primary aim in the minds of the conservative rulers. Despite their rhetoric, the war just begun did not seem to them to be fundamentally different from countless other wars they had survived.

What then does account for the expansion of the war? It is my thesis that the war became "total" mainly through its feedback effect on the domestic situation in France and not because of any conscious ideological aims entertained by either side from the out-set. As the war itself was a product of a revolutionary situation in France, the latter was to be influenced in turn by its own prod-uct. The war was revolutionized as a result of what is called the "Second Revolution" in France, an event which was in itself a product of the war. A vicious circle of war and revolution could not have a more telling illustration than in the case of the French Revolution.

It would be crude indeed to regard the war as "a ready-made explanation" for the Second Revolution.[1] On the other hand, it is also misleading to conclude that "how we judge the second revo-lution in France depends entirely on our judgment of the strength and chances, in 1792, of a Counter-Revolution aiming at integral restoration."[2] The point is not that the threat of a coun-terrevolution was real and imminent in 1792. It is rather that our explanation of the Second Revolution should be based on the perception of the situation by the very people who brought it about, and not on our own retrospective estimate of the "real" sit-uation. Men do not respond to reality as it really is, whatever that may mean, but rather to reality as they perceive it. The task of a sociologist is to establish the connections between perception and behavior, not to pronounce moral or political judgments.

How then did the French perceive their situation in the spring of 1792? The bad luck for the Revolution, which up to then had been relatively mild and might well have consolidated its achievement within the framework of a consitutional monar-chy, began with the fatal miscalculations of Dumouriez. As we have seen, Dumouriez, the self-appointed architect and executer of the war "on the House of Austria," had assumed from the be-ginning that both Britain and Prussia would remain neutral in a Franco-Austrian contest, an assumption more wishful than real. Britain under Pitt kept her formal neutrality, but disappointed Dumouriez by refusing even to receive his special envoy to Lon-don, Talleyrand, thus making it impossible to reach any "under-standing" regarding the future of Austria. As for Prussia, the so-called "traditional enmity" toward Vienna was conveniently forgotten in what promised to be a prelude to a quick and easy gain at the expense of revolutionary—hence disorganized—France. Was not France after all Austria's traditional ally? By weakening France, Prussia was sure that Austria too would suffer.

Under such circumstances, the only course of action open to Dumouriez seemed to be a decisive and speedy military action, accompanied by a cheap glory.[3] But the French could carry out this almost prophetic version of a blitzkrieg only with a considerable military superiority, which, as Lafayette had pointed out, was completely lacking.[4] The supply of men and materials constituted a serious problem in a revolutionary period; at the same time discipline, the essential condition for any army, was being replaced by extreme political agitation among the soldiers. As the officers were suspected of treason, the soldiers formed committees to protect themselves and the fatherland, linking themselves directly with civilian legislative bodies without the military superior's authorization. Patriotic manifestations became increasingly frequent when the national guards came into contact with the regular soldiers. Even the popular revolutionary societies were openly frequented by men in military uniforms. The breakdown of the military discipline became a foregone conclusion.[5]

As for the officers, they seem to have deserved the suspicion they received, for desertion of officers was a continuing, daily affair. The period between September 15 and December 1 alone saw 2,160 officers leave the Army and France.[6] Neither were the commanding generals in any better shape. They—Luckner, Rochambeau, and Lafayette—were far from being convinced of the efficacy of the unorthodox offensive strategy conceived by the adventurer Dumouriez. They were trained for regular orthodox military operations of the eighteenth-century type while for political reasons they decided not to invade at all.[7]

The invasion plan called for 50,000 men who would make up four columns. With the immediate objective of running over Belgium in a decisive and speedy action, it was proposed that the four columns, starting respectively from Dunkerque, Lille, Valenciennes, and Givet, should break through the enemy cordon on the 29th of April. On the day before the attack was to be mounted, however, an event took place that revealed only too painfully the true condition of the French army. A column on its way from Lille to Tournay was ordered to retreat by its commander, Téobald Dillon, who had very little heart for the offensive strategy to begin with, on the first sight of the Austrian troops. In retreat, the men, lacking any discipline, were immediately disbanded, and worse, cried "Treason." Dillon was murdered on the way back to Lille.[8]

When informed of the retreat, the Assembly responded by authorizing the government to make new regulations concerning *"le service interieur, la police et la discipline de l'infanterie."*[9] This act meant in effect that the Assembly was prepared to give up one of its most essential legislative functions only if by doing so it could aid the generals in winning the war.

The generals, however, were out of sympathy with the idea of a quick strike. They were conservative not only in their political aims but in their military methods as well. In their view, Dumouriez committed a fatal blunder in starting a war without even minimal preparations. What is amazing is that the generals did not conceal their contempt for Dumouriez. They declared jointly at Valenciennes on the 18th of May that the offensive plan as conceived by Dumouriez and now ordered by Servan, Minister of War, was absolutely impossible to carry out, and further blamed the failure of the first offensive on the lack of discipline in the Army.[10]

If the generals accepted the military failure calmly, almost relishing the opportunity it provided for blaming Dumouriez and his kind, the effect of the approaching German armies on the already excited Parisians was an entirely different matter, particularly as the military failure was compounded by an economic crisis.[11] The revolutionary imagination was easily persuaded of the existence of a clandestine committee that was allegedly passing millions to Austria, paying *émigrés,* causing the financial crisis deliberately by buying up the French market, and causing confusion by fabricating false paper money—as well as divulging French military plans to the enemies.[12] Popular suspicion was at first focused on two unimportant figures, Bertrand and Montmorin, who subsequently brought a suit against the imputations of treason which Carra in particular repeated most loudly in such papers as *Annales patriotique* and *Chronique de Paris*. Two days after the suit had been filed, on the 18th of May, Larivière, the justice of the peace who had received the complaint, had the nerve to issue a warrant against the so-called "Cordeliers Trio," namely Basire, Chabot, and Merlin de Thionville.[13] Larivière, however, could start his proceedings only with the Assembly's authorization, which was of course out of the question, since the Gironde-dominated Assembly would never allow its deputies to be prosecuted for having whipped the popular imagination by spreading suspicion of a clandestine committee. On the contrary, the only effect of the episode was to provide an occasion for Brissot to "prove" the existence of what was now called "the Austrian committee."[14]

It became quite obvious that the Girondin politicians were in a mood to exploit the popular sentiment. As a revolutionary party, it might be said, the Gironde was merely living up to its reputation by staking its destiny on the side of what after all a democratic consideration, namely the people's concern with national security. What the Girondins did not realize at the moment, of course, was that everything would depend on whether they were prepared to follow through the implications of their democratic (demagogic?) politics to their logical conclusion, for a popular sentiment tends to develop momentum of its own. The people who learned to sing the War Song of the Rhine Army, in which Rouget de Lisle, the author, succeeded in expressing nascent patriotism only too well, could not arbitrarily be stopped halfway before the patriotic passions had run their course. Having contributed to the irrevocable birth of modern nationalism, the Girondin politicians could retreat from the revolutionary tide only at the risk of revenge by the populace whose passion they had helped to incite for narrow political reasons. At the moment, however, it seemed that it was they, the Girondists, who were riding on top of the historical wave. It seemed always to be they who were on the offensive—or so they believed.

Under such circumstances, it was only natural that the Girondins should have produced what later historians have come to call three revolutionary decrees. First came the decree for the forced deportation of nonjuring priests, ostensibly for reasons of "public security and general police."[15] Two days later, on the 29th of May, the Assembly, dominated by the Girondins, took another revolutionary action by deciding to disband the King's bodyguard for "the personal security of the King and the public tranquillity."[16] Finally, on June 8, the Assembly voted to raise a new levee of 20,000 men, who would gather at Paris on Bastille Day and set up military camps of *Fédérés,* as they were called, in order "to remove every hope of the enemies of the public weal who are devising conspiracies in the interior. . . ."[17]

The real intention behind these decrees was quite clear. The *Fédérés* to be gathered at Paris were to be at the political disposal of the Girondins. Louis XVI, for all his publicized incompetence, knew that these revolutionary decrees were meant to make him even more a prisoner of the Girondins. Consenting only to disband his personal guard, the King found the nerve to veto both the bill against nonjuring priests and the plan for the military camp at Paris. When Roland, inspired by his wife, urged the King to accept the Assembly's decisions for fear of more violent consequences, Dumouriez was able to convince the King that Roland had to be dismissed from the ministry along with Clavière and Servan,[18] Servan to be replaced by Dumouriez himself as War Minister. The result of this intrigue and reshuffling was that Roland now became a hero with the Patriots, while Dumouriez lost all favor with the Assembly. Within a week of his appointment, Dumouriez had to resign his ministerial post and join the Army of the North.

Now the fall of the Girondin ministry was complete. When the King called in a purely Feuillant—that is, moderate—ministry, the impression was inescapable that the Court was plotting with the generals to break the power of the Jacobins, dismiss the Assembly, revise the Constitution, recall the *émigrés,* and stop the war by coming to terms with the enemy.[19] The popular suspicion was further strengthened by Lafayette's open letter to the Assembly urging the deputies to stop the radical democratic tide in order to protect their *"autorité légitime"* and *"le pouvoir roy-al."*[20] Vergniaud declared Lafayette's uninvited advice unconstitutional, while Gaudet compared the general to Cromwell. In any case, the general had made no small contribution to the already inflamed popular suspicion of a Court plot to undo the achievements of the Revolution.

As for the Girondins, it must be said that they had a rather moderating influence on the more radical elements of the Revolution, at least while they were in the ministry—but this was now over. The Parisian faubourgs were at last released into unchecked activism. On June 20, the crowd, gathered to celebrate the anniversary of the Tennis Court Oath, instead marched down to the Assembly where they read the so-called "Petition of June 20." Predictably, the petition spoke of the conspirators, the King's audacity in dismissing the patriotic ministers, the inaction of the armies, and the counterrevolutionary plot.[21] The crowd then broke into the Tuileries where they succeeded in forcing Louis XVI to pose wearing a red liberty cap. No violence occurred. The King, however, refused to recall the Girondin ministers, who subsequently persuaded the Assembly to pass a decree which authorized the *Fédérés* to come to Paris even against the King's will.[22] The Assembly had further responded to Brissot's demagogic demand by issuing on July 10 the often-cited declaration that *"la patrie est en danger."*

History, however, took one of those ironic turns at this point whereby the very fulfillment of ambition proves to be a fatal limitation. Just at the moment when the Girondins seemed to be leading the Revolution, their more secret ambition for the possession of the government was answered by the complete resignation of the Feuillant ministry. A new opportunity seemed to present itself for the Girondins to work amicably with the King. Indeed they lost no time in coming into contact with the King. Vergniaud, who had attacked the King for treason only two weeks before, now sent a secret letter to Louis through his court servants. Other letters followed. The King on his part was equal to the opportunity. He was determined to exploit the fluid situation to his own advantage—binding the Girondins' hands by extending a hope for a new ministerial appointment. Now, instead of attacking the throne, the Girondins suddenly came to its defense. Brissot spoke *"pour défendre la constitution et le trône,"* warning the people against "unconstitutional and unwise actions." The new slogan was to be *"la sagesse, la prudence et la réflexion la plus mûre,"*[23] which were hardly revolutionary notions. It became increasingly apparent that the Girondins were prepared to abandon their revolutionary career for the possession of what seemed to them a more tangible source of power, the government.

The result was a break between the Girondins on the one hand and the more radical elements on the other. The latter, largely made up of the *Fédérés* and the Parisian sans-culottes, could not easily be persuaded to liquidate their revolutionary enthusiasm, which was kindled so deliberately in the first place by the Girondins themselves. Even the slogan invented by the Girondins, *"la patrie est en danger,"* became the battle cry of excited masses.[24] To save the fatherland and the Revolution, which meant one and the same thing to them, the radical elements were prepared to go all the way, with or without the Girondins. In the end, Brissot and his cohorts would become the victims of their own designs.

It was against this explosive situation that the Duke of Brunswick at the head of the invading Prussian armies issued the famous Manifesto, urging the French to remain loyal to their King and receive the Prussian troops without any resistance. In the event the King or any member of the royal family were harmed or insulted, the German rulers, it was announced, would take an unprecedented, eternally memorable revenge by subjecting all of Paris to military execution.[25] The effect of the Manifesto, which reached Paris on August 1, was exactly the opposite of what its authors had hoped to accomplish by it. Both Baron Johannes Friedrich von Stein, who had first conceived of the Manifesto, and Frederick William, who enthusiastically approved the conception, shared with Louis and Marie-Antoinette the mistaken notion that such a declaration would prompt the more moderate Parisians to unite with the party of the center to avert the common calamity with which they were threatened.[26] Understandably enough, the

logic of incipient democratic nationalism was beyond the complacent imagination of these conservative men of routine. Instead of
being intimidated, as the authors of the Brunswick Manifesto had
hoped, the Parisians countered the German threat with a new decree promising French citizenship and a yearly pension to any
German deserter from the enemy line.[27] The dice were already
cast when Louis XVI, who had wanted something like the Manifesto of Brunswick, now tried to minimize its impact by expressing
his doubt about its authenticity.[28]

Perhaps a German observer exaggerated a bit when he wrote
from Paris that "the manifesto of the Duke of Brunswick toppled
Louis XVI from his throne."[29] But there can be no doubt that it
was this open threat from the Prussian commander combined with
the movement of the Prussian troops from Coblentz that gave an
apparent spontaneity to what would otherwise have required conscious justification. The passive citizens, whom the Manifesto was
intended to woo, could not now afford to oppose the more active
Patriots for fear of appearing to have been intimidated by the enemy's threat, or worse, even conspiring with the Germans against
"la patrie en danger." Now that the enemy committed the blunder of openly identifying its interest with that of Louis XVI, the
antimonarchical propaganda of the sans-culottes could appeal to
patriotism as well as to "liberty, equality, and fraternity." Democratic revolution—antimonarchical agitation—became thoroughly
mixed up with patriotism—resistance against the invading German troops. Patriotism came to mean the end of Louis XVI and
the monarchical regime.[30]

The monarchy was overthrown on August 10. Louis XVI was
to meet his end on January 21, 1793. In the meantime, the Revolution was not only saved from whatever real counterrevolutionary threat there was in the summer of 1792, but began to
assert itself with greater self-confidence against the crowned heads
of hostile Europe. If the ominous September massacres had eliminated all potential enemies within, the famous Battle of Valmy on
September 20 was the first of a series of successful military battles
to follow in the effort to eliminate all enemies without. Two days
after the stunning upset at Valmy, which Goethe, in a much-

quoted passage, described as epoch-making, the French Army under Montesquieu entered Montmelian and Chambery, the General being welcomed subsequently by the inhabitants of Savoy as their liberator. Similarly warm reception awaited when Anselme reached Nice on September 29. By the end of October, General Cultine had taken Spier, Worms, and Mainz, and pushing the Austrians across the Rhine, had finally entered Frankfurt-am-Main. The new Republic of France was obviously doing much better on the battlefield than the monarchy just overthrown.

But military success brought with it new problems, the most serious being treatment of the conquered territories. As Paris had not yet developed any clearly defined policy, the conquering generals were left very much to their own discretion. On the whole, they were proceeding to bring about either directly or indirectly what they considered to be a long-overdue democratizing revolution in each of the territories under their command. The question, therefore, naturally arose: Should the Convention declare for "liberation"? The so-called "patriots" of Nice, Savoy, and the Rhineland had already petitioned for "liberation" through annexation to France. There was also the example of Avignon, which had been annexed to France as early as September 1791. But Avignon was geographically inside French territory, whereas Nice and Savoy, parts of the Kingdom of Sardinia, were situated beyond existing French frontiers. The Convention was still divided between the advocates of "liberation" through annexation and those who tended to take a more cautious attitude for one reason or another.

Then came Dumouriez's brilliant victory at Jemapps on November 6, which, echoing the cannonade of Valmy, was followed by his subsequent seizure of Brussels and conquest of the Austrian Netherlands. The heady excitement of such an easy military success would be difficult for even the more cautious to resist. For the deputies of the Assembly, who were already feeling the expansive spirit of a revolution that had been accomplished, Jemappes destroyed all lingering doubt about the wisdom of pursuing "liberation" through annexation. Once again, as happens so often in history, a military accident dictated the course of political life. On

November 19, the Convention promised "fraternity and aid to all peoples who wished to recover their liberty." A week later, on November 27, this promise was fulfilled when the Convention, with only two dissenting votes, decided to annex Savoy as the eighty-fourth department of the Republic of France. As the Abbé Grégoire, who moved for annexation of Savoy, made clear, the reasons for this first act of truly revolutionary expansion were quite mixed: besides the noble objective of liberating the people of Savoy from their "tyrant," annexation was demanded in the name of geography, common interests, and circumstances of war.[31]

However, the task of "liberation" was not to be limited to Savoy alone. There was no concealing the ultimate objective, which seemed to be nothing short of liberating all of Europe from the crowned "tyrants." As Brissot, the foremost champion of revolutionary expansionism, argued on November 26, the newly born Republic of France, engaged as it was in a struggle with the "Germanic colossus," could not be "at ease until Europe, and all Europe, is in flames." Demanding the Rhine frontier as a "natural part of France," Brissot thundered, "Our liberty will never rest quietly as long as a Bourbon is enthroned. There can be no peace with Bourbon: with that understood, we must consider an expedition into Spain."[32]

There seems to have been something like a genuine popular desire for annexation to France among the inhabitants of Savoy and Nice, but such certainly was not the case in Belgium and the Rhineland.[33] It was therefore quite obvious that these peoples, and many others, if they were to share the taste of liberty with the French, had to be forced to become free. France could no longer remain content with general promises and mere willingness to take them in if and when they requested. It was necessary to bring them into the bosom of the land of liberty through more active and specific steps. These were provided by the often-cited Decree of December 15. In it the Convention declared that in all the countries which were or would be occupied by the armies of the French Republic, the generals should immediately proclaim the sovereignty of the people, the suppression of all the established authorities, and the abolition of all existing taxes and revenues, of the tithe and the corvée, of exclusive hunting rights, and all other privileges of nobility. It was further decided that the generals should immediately convoke the people in primary assemblies in order to create and organize a provisional administration.

These were clearly far-reaching revolutionary measures. In retrospect, it is easy to discern their fundamentally ideological character. Their motivations, however, were quite mixed. For one thing, the Convention seems to have supposed that one method of saving the declining assignat (paper money issued by the Revolutionary Government) was to use it in payment for confiscated properties. For another thing, it is quite probable, as Chuquet argued, that the Convention believed that these political measures provided the best means of controlling the generals at the front who had previously lacked any concrete instructions from Paris regarding treatment of the conquered territories. Whatever their true intentions, the chief effect of the Decree of December 15 was to alienate the peoples whose properties were being arbitrarily confiscated in exchange for the assignats, which were generally believed to be worthless.

Alienation notwithstanding, the French did not hesitate to proceed with the policy of "liberation," starting with the annexation of Nice on January 31, 1793, then the annexation of Belgium on the basis of "elections" supervised by French agents and their Belgian followers[34] in the following month, and in March that of the Rhineland to complete the annexationist phase of the Girondin regime. Thus overextended beyond the limits of its physical power, France subsequently met the inevitable reverse of its military fortune. On March 18, the Austrians under the Duke of Coburg defeated Dumouriez at Neerwinden and went on to recapture Brussels. This decisive defeat of Dumouriez and his subsequent defection to the Austrian side was to spell the end of the Girondins, a development which will be taken up in a separate chapter.

•   •   •

In less than a year, a war which most of the French people regarded as defensive in purpose was turned into an ideological crusade to free Europe from its "tyrants." What brought about this change? What prevented the war of 1792 from remaining a limited contest for limited stakes in the tradition of the classical balance-of-power system?

The motives of the Girondin leaders, who were more responsible than anyone else for the expansionism of France in the fall of 1792, were quite mixed. To begin with, as in most aggressive acts of any state, the expansionist policy of the French Republic had its own share of rational considerations that were allegedly based on the requirements of France's national security. Carnot, whom Napoleon was to call "organizer of victory," argued in the Diplomatic Committee of the Convention that "annexation" was "indispensable" for "the general safety of the Republic." To secure the latter, he proposed that the Republic should recover and maintain "the ancient and natural boundaries of France," which in his view were "the Rhine, the Alps, and the Pyrenees."[35] Lebrun, Minister of Foreign Affairs, subscribed wholeheartedly to this "natural boundary" theory.[36] On the surface, therefore, the expansionism of the Girondin regime seems to have been essentially in the same category as the age-old ambition of France under the Bourbons to extend its sphere of power and glory; the monarchy too held the so-called "natural-boundary" view, which was allegedly based on what had been presumably the rightful territory of ancient Gaul. But such an impression does not take account of the impact the Revolution had on French political thinking in this as in other areas. The fact is that the old monarchy, while ambitious in its territorial policy, did not find the concept of "nature" implicit in the natural-boundary theory particularly convincing.[37] Was it not after all Rousseau, the spiritual father of the democratic revolution, who had advanced the natural-boundary theory most eloquently? It was left to the leaders of the Republic to discover the special charm of "natural" frontiers which accorded so perfectly with the new concept of Nature as a governing principle of an ideal society. Even the language of national security, when spoken by the men engaged in remaking France and possibly Europe as well, could not but be colored by their ideological convictions.

Their ideological commitment was to a world of transnational goals. As early as 1790, the new representatives of the
French people had declared: "The French Nation renounces the
undertaking of any war with a view to making conquests, and it
will never use its forces against the liberty of any people." Such
declarations of pacific intentions would be harmless enough, were
it not for the fact that its logical corollary could only be that any
military victory achieved by the peace-loving Republic must mean
the opposite of conquest, namely "liberation." To many excited
revolutionaries, it came to seem axiomatic that the French soldiers should be welcomed as liberators, since they were engaged in
"wars against chateaux" and in bringing "peace to cottages."
That such a happy coincidence of France's material interest (security through "natural frontiers") with humanity's spiritual
need ("liberation") might be due to an illusion was not
seriously considered. Indeed it is a rare revolutionary who in the
moment of his triumph willingly casts doubt on the validity of his
own convictions. Even rarer is a nation that can, in an hour of its
military success, subject its own ambitions and aims to a cool and
critical examination. After all, the military achievements of the
newly born Republic, upsetting all the traditional calculations of
military power, seemed to prove nothing less than that a nation
on the side of "liberty" was indeed invincible. The tide of history
seemed to be turning just as Condorcet had predicted.

If there was any need to bolster this sense of a universal mission among the French, there were gathered in Paris enough foreign revolutionaries to do just that. Without actually causing the
expansionism of France, the total effect of their varied intrigues
and lobbying activities was nevertheless to strengthen the French
conviction that Europe was more "ripe" for a democratic revolution than it really was. To be sure, as recent historical works by
Godechot and Palmer make clear, Europe and not just France
alone experienced something like a pervasive democratic mood.[38]
But the point here is not that the French Revolution tried to impose itself upon a completely unwilling world. It is rather that the
men of 1792 were engaged in spreading the Revolution out of a
conviction that the peoples everywhere longed to be "liberated"

from their "tyrants." We are here concerned with the motivation of the expansionists, not the reality of democratic stirrings in countries other than France.

More interesting, however, than the question of motivation is the question of occasion: What made the expansionism of 1792 possible? Given the motivation, it is still necessary to ask: What factors specifically made it possible to translate the intentions of some into reality for all? The latter question is all the more intriguing since there was, as we saw, very little in the Revolution of 1789 to make the expansionism of 1792 "inevitable."

Historians are understandably skeptical of hypothetical speculations. But to a sociologist interested in discovering patterns and their underlying causes, consideration of "possibilities"[39] is indispensable. The ideological expansion of a war begun so inauspiciously should be regarded, therefore, not as the only possible outcome of the Revolution but rather as one of many possibilities even within the context of the Revolution in France. To be sure, the ingredients were all there. Revolutionary ideology, military technology, new strategic concepts, rising nationalism, and necessary actors were all present, impinging upon the inevitably fragile international system at the turn of the century. We are mainly interested, however, in the mix of these ingredients rather than the elements themselves. How one factor influenced the others to produce something different from any of them—this is the main object of our analysis.

We have already seen how the introduction of one ideologically dissimilar actor led to the increasing malfunctioning of the communications network among international actors. Decision-making in France was no longer the old familiar routine entrusted mainly to select official agents. In a developing revolutionary situation, the King and his ministers were constantly being pushed out of their former control over France's foreign policy by the rising pressure from below. This breakdown of a stable decision-making process in France might have had only a limited impact on international stability if the other powers had understood the dynamics of a revolutionary situation and acted accordingly. Such intellectual capacity was conspicuous by its absence. The conservatives persisted in seeing the Revolution through their own familiar glasses, which meant that they could respond to the events in France only within the traditional framework of the balance-of-power system. The effect on France of conservative responses from without was to aggravate further her already revolutionary situation within. The result was a war between France and Austria, involving Prussia automatically as the latter's ally.

Pushing our hypothetical speculation one step further, it is entirely possible to think that the war of 1792 might have remained an orthodox operation of the familiar variety. What prevented such development was most likely the revolutionary transformation of the Revolution itself. The war contributed decisively to the failure of the monarchical experiment, which in turn revolutionized the war. The dialectic of war and revolution came full circle from the latter producing the former to the former affecting the latter. In the language of systems analysis, it might be said that the revolutionary expansion of the war was mainly due to the feedback effect of the war on one of the primary actors of the international system.

Feedback is of course never automatic. Its net effect depends on many things, among them the nature of the variable being affected. The exigencies of a war may or may not produce irrevocable transformations in the structure of a political system. It was largely the revolutionary condition of French society itself that determined the particular outcome of external disturbances to the French political system. In other words, France in the spring and summer of 1792 did not possess an adaptive mechanism which could withstand the shocks administered to her by a series of military failures. The Second Revolution was a product of interaction between the external and internal factors, and not of one or the other, as some historians seem to feel the case should be.

The relevant aspect of the internal situation in France was the extreme degree to which foreign-policy decisions became subject to popular pressure. The Girondists had done their share to bring about such a situation, but, as we saw, in the end they too were unable to control the popular movement toward increasing radicalism, a movement which the Jacobins or the Mountain stood to exploit in their power struggle against the Brissotins. If we concentrate on the details of domestic struggle for power, however, it is easy to lose sight of the forest for the trees. Essentially, the striking fact was that ordinary citizens of France became a formidable factor in the affairs of the state for the first time. The so-called "reason of state" which used to be the exclusive province of the sovereigns was no longer narrowly identified with the interest and judgment of the crown. After all, the Revolution had ushered in a new era in 1789. A certain degree of democratization was to be expected.

Ultimately, the democratic revolution would reduce the level of France's internalized acceptance of the normative restraints inherent in the old order of international relations. Sovereignties would matter less, insofar as they were defined in terms of dynastic interests and powers. Instead would arise a new concept of popular sovereignty. This process of the rise of popular sovereignty was curiously enough a product of the workings of the old international system itself in a new environment. Being unable to cope with the new revolutionary challenge, the international system was hastening its own collapse by influencing one of its essential units in a revolutionary direction.

Our analysis raises a fundamental question of statesmanship in a revolutionary age. If the limited perspective of conservative rulers contributed decisively to the progressive aggravation of the domestic revolutionary process within France, thereby helping to bring about the collapse of the old order in international relations as well, was it really possible for them to act in such a way as to prevent the final disintegration of a more or less familiar system of decision-making in France? A more extended treatment of this problem will have to wait for the analysis of later developments. Tentatively, it can be suggested that at least they could have minimized the impact of external factors on the French political system either by acting in such a manner as to create some sense of security among the French, entailing acceptance of the Revolution without provocative rhetoric against it, or by launching a truly effective counterrevolutionary crusade from the outset, as Burke had advocated. In 1792, neither course of action was seriously contemplated. Instead, half-hearted measures, mostly inconsequential in defeating France, had the unintended effect of identifying the Revolution with patriotism in the eyes of even ordinary Frenchmen. The rise of nationalism in France was therefore decisively aided by the blunders committed by conservatives, who could not free themselves from the traditional obsession with limited territorial aims and tactical advantages. Their limited vision, together with the already explosive situation in France, did much to insure the collapse of the old international relations.

Notes

1. Crane Brinton, *op. cit.,* p. 95.
2. R. R. Palmer, *The Age of the Democratic Revolution,* Vol. II, p. 36.
3. Albert Sorel, *op. cit.,* Vol. II, pp. 437–456.
4. Lafayette went further, probably out of political motives. Entrusted with one of the three armies for the invasion task, he wrote to de Grave: *"Je ne puis concevoir comment on a pu déclarer la guerre, en nétant rien."* Lafayette to de Grave, 11 Aug.–2 Sept., 1792, quoted by A. Chuquet, *Les Guerres de la Révolution* (Paris, 1886–1896), Vol. I, p. 24.
5. A. Chuquet, *op. cit.,* Vol. I, Chap. II.
6. P.-J.-B. Buchez and P.-C. Roux, *Histoire parlementaire de la Révolution française, ou Journal des assemblées nationales depuis 1789 jusqu'en 1815* (Paris, 1834–1838), Vol. II, p. 387. Hereafter referred to as *Histoire parlementaire.*
7. Cf. Ramsay Weston Phipps, *The Armies of the First French Republic and the Rise of the Marshals of Napoleon,* Vol. I: *The Armée du Nord* (Oxford, 1926), pp. 84–85. See also Henry Jomini, *Histoire critique et militaire des guerres de la Révolution* (Paris, 1819–1824), Vol. II, pp. 18–19.
8. Henry Jomini, *op. cit.,* Vol. II, pp. 14–18. General Biron also ordered retreat at the first sight of the enemy, while Carle and Lafayette did not even spot the enemy before turning back.
9. *Archives parlementaires,* Vol. XLIII, p. 6. See also *Moniteur,* Vol. XII, pp. 271–272.
10. A. Chuquet, *op. cit.;* Dumouriez, p. 84.
11. Albert Mathiez, *La vie chère et le mouvement social sous la Terreur* (Paris, 1927), Chaps. I and II.
12. H. A. Goetz-Bernstein, *La Diplomatie de la Gironde: Jacques-Pierre Brissot* (Paris, 1912), pp. 206–221.
13. *Histoire parlementaire,* Vol. XIV, p. 278.

14. *Archives parlementaires, Vol.* XLIV, pp. 33–43; also *Moniteur,* Vol. XII, pp. 442–443.

15. J. B. M. Duvergier, ed., *Collection complet des lois, décrets, ordonnances, règlements et avis du Conseil d'Etat de 1788 à 1824,* continued by annual volumes thereafter (Paris, 1824–1878), Vol. IV, pp. 177–178.

16. *Ibid.,* Vol. IV, pp. 180–181. For debates on these decrees, see *Moniteur,* Vol. XII, p. 490, and also *Archives parlementaires,* Vol. XLIV, p. 305.

17. *Moniteur,* Vol. XII, p. 607.

18. Frederic Masson, *Le Département des affaires étrangères pendant la Révolution, 1787–1804* (Paris, 1877, p. 178.

19. Albert Mathiez, *The French Revolution* (New York, 1928), p. 152.

20. *Archives parlementaires,* Vol. XLV, pp. 338–340.

21. *Moniteur,* Vol. XII, p. 717.

22. *Ibid.,* Vol. XIII, p. 24.

23. *Ibid.,* Vol. XIII, p. 253.

24. See, for example, the so-called "Adresse du conseil général de la commune de Marseilles," in *Archives parlementaires,* Vol. XLVI, pp. 383–384; also the statement of the *Fédérés,* in *ibid.,* Vol. XLVII, pp. 67–70.

25. *Histoire parlementaire,* Vol. XVI, p. 276.

26. J. Hansen, ed., *op. cit.,* Vol. II, p. 298. See also Marie-Antoinette to de Mercy, July 4, 1792, in A. R. von Arneth, *op. cit.,* p. 265.

27. *Moniteur,* Vol. XIII, pp. 311–312.

28. *Ibid.,* Vol. XIII, pp. 323–324.

29. G. Landauer, ed., *Briefe aus der Französischen Revolution* (Frankfurt-am-Main, 1919), Vol. II, p. 302, quoted by S. Biro, *op. cit.,* Vol. I, p. 70.

30. See the Address of the Paris sections, which may be regarded as the manifesto of Aug. 10. *Archives parlementaires,* Vol. XLVII, pp. 425–427.

31. *Moniteur,* Vol. XIV, p. 587.

32. J.-P. Brissot, *Correspondance et papiers* (Paris, 1919), pp. 304, 313 ff.

33. On Belgium, see Suzanne Tassier, *Histoire de la Belgique sous l'occupation française en 1792 et 1793* (Brussels, 1934). On the Rhineland, see S. Biro, *op. cit.,* Vol. I, pp. 103–144.

34. I am following Tassiers view on this, which is contested by R. R. Palmer in *The Age of Democratic Revolution,* Vol. II, p. 81.

35. E. Charavay, ed., *Correspondance général de Carnot* (Paris, 1892–1907), Vol. I, pp. 369–370.

36. J. Hansen, *op. cit.,* Vol. II, pp. 541–542.

37. G. Zeller argued that the *ancien régime* never committed itself wholeheartedly to the natural frontier theory. See "La Monarchie d'ancien régime et les frontières naturelles," *Revue d'histoire modern,* Vol. XIII (1963).

38. See particularly R. R. Palmer, "Reflections on the French Revolution," *Political Science Quarterly,* LXVII (1952).

39. Max Weber maintained that every historical work worthy of publication should contain "judgments of possibilities." *Methodology of the Social Sciences,* trans. by Edward A. Shils and Henry A. Finch (New York, 1949), p. 173.

IV

The Failure of the First Coalition:
The Limits of Conservative Policy in a Revolutionary Age

If the old order in international relations was already deep in the process of dissolution by the fall of 1792, those most clearly destined to suffer from its consequences did not know it yet. Despite her exhortations for a crusade against the Revolution, the Russian Tzarina, Catherine II, was more concerned with Poland than France, while the Kings of Sweden and Spain, two singularly devoted champions of the ancient regime, were powerless to do anything about the Revolution by themselves. If there was to be a general European action against the Revolution, it was only England that could provide initiative and leadership.

But Edmund Burke, who had already proposed a crusade against "an irrational, unprincipled, proscribing, confiscating, plundering, ferocious, bloody, and tyrannical democracy,"[1] was almost alone in England in seeing the French Revolution in ideological terms. Neither Pitt nor his cousin Grenville, in charge of foreign affairs, saw any point in acting prematurely against France. Their confidence in the strength of British institutions was stronger than their fear of whatever menace the Revolution posed to the domestic tranquility within England. So too was the confidence of George III in his own ministers unshakable, while his intense personal dislike for Burke was no secret. In any case, as Grenville wrote to Auckland in June of 1792, England did not have even the slightest doubt about the outcome of the war between France and the German coalition, and "as soon as the Ger-

man troops arrive in Paris," it seemed certain that "whatever is
the ruling party in Paris must apply to [London] to mediate for
them."[2] Confident of the German military superiority, the British were preparing themselves to play the familiar role of a me-
diator among continental rival powers. What Pitt and Grenville
failed to realize was that Britain's traditional role as a "balancer"
could be played successfully only within the framework of a balance-of-power system. But the truth was that it was no longer
marginal adjustments within the system that required England's
response. Faced with a radical and fundamental challenge, the
system could be saved only by its members' acting beyond the
usual limits of ordinary behavior. To do so would have required a
more imaginative understanding of the dynamic nature of the
Revolution and its disruptive impact on international life than
was available to such men as Pitt and Grenville, who were conservative by temperament as well as conviction.

To be sure, England's policy of neutrality had one more
premise, which, if realized fully, might have become a viable
basis for a more creative response to the revolutionary challenge.
As Lord Grenville wrote, England seems to have believed that
"foreign intervention [would serve] the cause of anarchy by giving both an excuse for its disorders and the means of collecting
military force to support them [in France]."[3] The inevitable
conclusion would then have been acceptance of the Revolution, at
least as it was declared "over" in the fall of 1791 by no less a
figure than Louis XVI himself.[4] If consideration of the possible
effect of counterrevolutionary action on the domestic politics of
France was the fundamental premise of Britain's policy, not only
should she have abstained herself, but also attempted to discour-
age the German powers from going to war against France. By ex-
pecting the German troops to accomplish what England herself
was reluctant to undertake, Pitt was basically inconsistent. Only
by making a clear choice between acceptance or rejection of the
Revolution, could England have made a creative contribution to
the task of stabilizing European relations.

Pitt was not thinking along these fundamental lines. He was
incapable of recognizing the novelty of the challenge presented

by the French Revolution. He was therefore determined to respond to it within the framework of the traditional balance-of-
power system, which linked British security to certain concrete
territorial controls and not to illusive ideological symbols. Thus
he did not hesitate to declare as early as 1789 that only a French
invasion of the Belgian provinces would definitely constitute a
casus belli for Great Britain.[5]

It was in November 1792 that France, now a Republic, provided the explicit occasion for British intervention. Having defeated in the meantime the approaching Prussian troops at
Valmy and Jemappes, the French were now marching out in the
intoxication of easy victory and popular enthusiasm. Even Robespierre did not try to stem the tide. If Burke was wrong in 1791 in
thinking that revolutionary France meant to upset the whole of
Europe, France under the Convention was doing everything to
prove him right in the fall of 1792. Thus on the 16th of November,
while the Convention was debating the question of annexation in
the name of bringing liberty to the newly emancipated peoples,
its Executive Committee decided that exclusive control of the
Scheldt and the Meuse by the Dutch Republic was in violation of
the fundamental principles of natural law, although the Dutch
controlled the waters in accordance with the terms of the Treaty
of Westphalia. The Council therefore instructed the commanding
general in charge of the French armies in the Belgium expedition
to assure the freedom of the navigation of the Scheldt and the
Meuse even at the risk of a military action.[6]

On the same fateful day, Britain sent a declaration to the
States-General of the United Provinces, giving "the assurance of
[His Majesty's] inviolable friendship, and of his determination to
execute, at all times, with the utmost good faith, all the different
stipulations of the Treaty of Alliance so happily concluded, in
1788, between his Majesty and their High Mightiness."[7] Grenville,
lacking even the slightest insight into the dynamics of a revolutionary power, hoped to the last moment that such a declaration of a
firm intent on the part of Britain would have a deterring effect upon the French, while bolstering the Dutch morale.[8] He was, of
course, mistaken. The French Republic could retract its decree of

November 16 only at the risk of losing prestige as well as giving
comfort and confidence to the German powers with whom she
was already at war. If England could never allow the estuary of
the Scheldt to fall into the hands of a rival power, neither could
France afford to withdraw from her own action in this eleventh
hour without grave consequences. The dice were cast. It was
therefore utterly in vain that Grenville demanded of Chauvelin
on November 29 that the edict of November 16 be revoked. Instead of revoking the decree for free navigation of the Scheldt
estuary, the French Convention ordered on December 15 the suppression of all existing authorities in the districts occupied by the
French troops, inviting the liberated peoples to accept the principles of liberty and equality and advising them to form provisional governments on these bases.[9] If the war began without
clearly defined ideological aims, it was acquiring them rapidly.

In the meantime, democratic agitation was growing at a menacing pace within England itself. Popular associations dedicated
to democratic propaganda were becoming more restive as economic conditions became worse. Furthermore, despite the September massacre, the Revolution's military victories in the fall
apparently gave new heart to the democrats already committed to
its cause, who were scheduled to meet in a general assembly
on December 11. Actually the threat to "the tranquility and continued existence of cherished English institutions"[10] could not
have been really alarming, but there was enough agitation to
convince Grenville that the French were committed to subvert
within as well as attack from without.[11] Even to the stiff mind of
complacent Grenville, the ideological character of the crisis was
becoming undeniable.

War preparations began to be made in England as Pitt called
up the militia on December 1 and had the Alien Bill passed on
December 31. In January the government halted all shipments of
grain and raw materials to the French Republic. When Louis
XVI, whose fate curiously did not seem to matter in the determination of British policy, was tried before the Convention and exe-
cuted on January 21, 1793, Britain reacted by ordering the
withdrawal of Chauvelin from the realm within eight days. When

Chauvelin arrived in Paris on February 1, the Convention voted for a declaration of war against England. The war would have broken out even without the King's execution, but the latter hastened what would have occurred in any case.

Once at war, Britain resorted naturally enough to her traditional method of fighting a continental enemy: As an insular power, she would have her war fought by other continental powers. Thus, on the 25th of March, 1793, Grenville and Vorontzoff signed a treaty of alliance between Great Britain and Russia whereby the latter promised to use her forces along with those of Great Britain against the French Republic. Other similar treaties followed. On April 25 one with Sardinia, May 25 with Spain, July 12 with Naples, July 14 with Prussia, August 30 with Austria, and September 26 with Portugal.[12] The substances of the agreements were virtually the same. Each contracting power promised to furnish a certain specified number of troops in return for British subsidies, giving the "alliance" a somewhat mercenary character. At last, however, there emerged something approaching a European coalition of the crowned heads against the regicidal Republic of France.

The military superiority of the Coalition was overwhelming from a purely material point of view. The French forces were still in a hazardous state of confusion, while the Coalition had at its disposal 55,000 Austrian soldiers amassed near the Rhine, 11,000 Prussians under the celebrated Duke of Brunswick, 13,000 Hanoverians to the right of the Austrians, 33,000 Prussians under Hohenlohe-Kirchberg in reserve, and 42,000 of Frederick William's own troops, plus reinforcement of 14,000 other German troops, ready for the invasion of eastern France. Without even counting 120,000 more promised by the Holy Roman Empire, the number of the Coalition forces seemed large enough to assure a quick end to the revolutionary drive of the French Republic.

Such, however, was not the result of the actual engagements —indeed the outcome was exactly the contrary of what the initial superiority of the Coalition forces would have led one to anticipate. After a few initial victories, the first Coalition collapsed without translating its superior military potential into an actual triumph. The Austrian victory under the Duke of Coburg at Neerwinden on March 18, 1793, was followed by the Battle of Fleurus on June 26 in the following year, which marked a turning point in the military career of the French Republic—now reorganized for triumph through the genius of Caron. The Austrians were forced to yield Belgium to the French again. Retreat of the allied forces across the Rhine became general by December of 1793. The French captured Worms and Spier, and forced the British out of Toulon.[13] And by the 5th of April in 1795, the Coalition came to its virtual end, as in the first treaty of Basel Prussia signed its peace with France.

By the treaty, France was assured of the left bank of the Rhine until peace should be concluded with the Empire, evacuating presently only the right bank, and northern Germany was to be neutralized. By its secret articles, Prussia consented to the absolute cession of the left bank to France and was in return given French assurance of compensation through secularization of ecclesiastical territory on the right bank. Saxony, Hanover, and Hesse-Cassel were by now also at peace with France. On June 22, Spain too concluded peace with France at Basel, ceding Santo Domingo in return for other lost territories which were to be restored. The French Republic, which seemed to be doomed to a catastrophic defeat at the advent of the first European Coalition, was now saved, and what is more astonishing, took the historical initiative into its own hands, commanding the fate of the European community for a decade until the young artillery officer of the Toulon campaign could be subdued.

How did this reversal of anticipation come about? Why and how was the military superiority of the Coalition turned into a defeat and finally the dissolution of the Coalition itself? The answer lies in the nature of the war aims separately entertained by the Allies. From the outset, there were two possible conceptions of war aims. One, advocated by Burke and Gustavus III of Sweden, would have regarded the restoration of the old regime in France as the primary task of the conservative Coalition. The alternative consisted in a war within the traditional framework of the balance-of-power system, in which marginal gains in territory and other properties were of supreme importance, for the basic equilibrium was assumed to be more or less permanent.

The first choice could have been fulfilled only if the French Revolution had been regarded as enough of a threat to the international system itself for the conservative powers to suspend, at least temporarily, their traditional concern with limited gains and losses and join instead in the common task of defeating the revolutionary challenge. Such was not the goal nor intention of the successful statesmen of dynastic politics. Despite repeated protestations of their determination to defeat the revolutionary menace now threatening the stability of the entire European civilization, the fact was that their actual concerns were invariably fixed within the range of values defined by the conservative system.

Thus it was that the Empress of Russia, while sparing no rhetoric in warning Europe of the Jacobin menace, was actually more concerned to divert the attentions of the German courts away from eastern Europe. It was there that she had concrete designs, while the spread of the Revolution was still only a theoretical threat to the Russian Empire. Catherine's ambition with respect to gaining Polish territory had been further kindled by the Constitution of May 3, 1791, which, by abolishing the incapacitating *liberum veto,* seemed to promise a reformed and independent Poland. The Russian court naturally took this prospect as conclusive evidence that Poland should by no means be left alone. As a first step, Catherine II succeeded in inducing a group of reactionary Polish nobles to form the Confederation of Targowica in May, 1792, which, with the aid of Russian troops, began the invasion of Poland.

In turn, the King of the Hohenzollerns was understandably alarmed at the prospect of Russian strength menacing Prussian territory without the protection of Poland as a buffer zone. The Russian move seemed to have caught the Prussians at a particularly bad moment, as Berlin was just commencing a campaign against France. The only alternative open to the Prussian monarch seemed to be that of coming to terms with the Russian court. Thus came about the secret treaty of Polish partition that was signed between Russia and Prussia at St. Petersburg on the

23rd of January, 1793.[14] Ironically enough, partition was justified in the name of "order" and "the general tranquility," which were said to be threatened by "the fatal revolution in France." In more substantial terms, Russia acquired the Polish territories east of the Druja-Pinsk-Choczim line, that is, virtually the whole eastern half of the Polish Republic. Territories bounded by the Czestochowa-Rawa-Soldau line, namely the whole of Great Poland, went to Prussia. One condition for Prussia's acquisition of the partitioned Polish territory, however, was that the war against France should be continued, while Russia was not obliged to take part in it. On the face of it, this would seem unfair to Prussia. Actually, though, the Prussian pledge to continue the war had an escape clause. A stipulation had been deliberately inserted by the Prussian ministry to the effect that Prussia would carry on the war against the French Republic "in common with the Emperor," for Berlin assumed, not without reason, that the Emperor would seize the first opportunity to wash his hands of the French involvement. This tangled web of assumptions and presuppositions contained of course the very seed of destruction for the Coalition itself. Within the framework of the traditional balance-of-power system, however, nothing could have been more natural than that sovereign states should have been primarily concerned with territorial adjustments most likely to affect their physical security.

At any rate, on the day immediately following the signing of the St. Petersburg Convention, the Prussian troops under General Mollendorff began the occupation of eastern Poland, which naturally aroused apprehension in the Viennese court. What made matters worse for the Austrians was that the Convention of St. Petersburg had been kept secret from them at the explicit instruction of the Empress. It was not until March 5 that Louis Cobenzle, the Austrian ambassador at the Russian court, could report even that such a treaty had been signed; its contents remained unknown to the Austrians until the Russian court communicated them directly to Vienna on March 23.[15] In the meantime, the Emperor remained committed without reservation to the Belgic-Bavarian Exchange Plan, to which the Tzarina gave full support while Prussia consented to it only grudgingly on the condition of Austria's acquiescence in the Polish partition.

London, however, expressed through Lord Grenville its objection to the Bavarian Exchange Plan and in its place held out hopes that, if the Emperor would renounce the exchange of Belgium for Bavaria and promise to retain Belgium, England might gladly help him acquire an indemnity at the expense of France, probably Lille and Valenciennes.[16] In view of this British attitude, and especially now that the contents of the St. Petersburg Convention had become known to the Viennese court, it was imperative for the Emperor to reconsider thoroughly the entire line of diplomacy as conducted up to that time by the ministry of Philip Cobenzle. Such a critical task fell upon Baron von Thugut.

In his Memorial presented sometime in March of 1793, the Baron had already criticized the Bavarian Exchange Plan, a conception of Cobenzle whose understanding of diplomacy flatly contradicted the tradition signified by the name of von Kaunitz. Thugut argued that it was not only demoralizing but essentially too precarious to base a general system of Austrian foreign policy on a plan which depended for its execution on the will of Prussia—and therefore could not possibly be ensured. Had not Prussia already violated the most essential stipulation of the alliance, namely *"une égalité parfaite dans toutes les vues d'agrandissement et d'acquisitions respectives des deux cours"*?[17] To rely on Prussia after such a clear exhibition of bad faith would be sheer folly, according to Thugut. Austria, instead, should endeavor to find her indemnification in another plan that would be less complicated and consequently less contingent. The Baron concluded by arguing that to balance the selfish aggrandizement of Prussia in Poland, the Emperor should aim at conquests in France. Such could best be accomplished by closer alliance with England combined with vigorous execution of war against France, and by freeing Austria from the dangerous reliance on the unpredictable Prussian court.

Thugut's arguments were cogent, forceful, and persuasive. The Emperor was convinced that the system of Cobenzle and Spielmann, based on the repudiation of the traditional enmity between Prussia and Austria, had come to complete bankruptcy. On March 27, Cobenzle and Spielmann received cordial notes from the Emperor dismissing them from their ministerial posts. Baron von Thugut, a faithful pupil of von Kaunitz, succeeded immediately as *"directeur général du bureau des affaires étrangères."* And in the person of Thugut Austria found one of the most complete and efficient products of the cynical eighteenth-century diplomacy for which that country became famous. Henceforth, the war against France would be conducted as part of a more general policy aimed at the European balance of power.

More concretely, Thugut's policy consisted in two simultaneous efforts. First, attempts were made to induce Russia and Prussia to modify their St. Petersburg Convention so as to guarantee serving the Imperial interests through a corresponding indemnification somewhere, the territories for it being deliberately left undefined.[18] The second effort was to ally Austria with England in such a way that intrigues with London would compel Russia and Prussia to pay a significant price for Austria's indispensable (as he hoped) cooperation in the final consummation of the Polish partition—to which, then, Austria would give her consent only on certain conditions.[19] Both policies were based on the conception expounded in the Memorial, namely the principle of *"une scrupuleuse égalité dans les avantages réciproques."*

The effect of Thugut's policy was first felt at the Congress of Antwerp on April 17, 1793. At its first sitting, the Congress considered the April 5 Manifesto of the Duke of Coburg, who was urged by Dumouriez to renounce publicly any allied territorial ambitions at the expense of France. Dumouriez, having failed at Paris, now argued that with such a declaration by the Allies he could easily procure the cooperation of the French people in the Allied cause. In all probability Dumouriez could not have succeeded in this enterprise. That the Manifesto of April 5 would have had less damaging effect than the one subsequently issued from Antwerp, however, is scarcely doubtful. Since Austria had already decided that she should carve out her share of "advantages" at the expense of France, a policy which England also preferred to the Belgic-Bavarian Exchange Plan, the Congress of Antwerp endorsed a new declaration drawn up by Metternich repudiating explicitly the good intentions vouchsafed by the Duke of Coburg in the April 5 Manifesto. Coburg was obliged to publish the Antwerp declaration on April 19, turning the war against France into a war of sheer territorial conquest.

The impact of the Antwerp declaration on the French people was similar to that of the Manifesto of Brunswick: Both had aroused the French people's dormant nationalism by threatening an invasion without actually carrying it out. No more effective means could have been found to solidify the achievement of the Revolution within France and imbue its champions everywhere with a sense of righteous indignation. But perhaps the more disastrous consequence was that the Allies entrapped themselves in what one of the participants had called in one of his more lucid moments a diplomatic "labyrinthe."[20] Still deep in the tradition of classical diplomacy, the conservative powers were chiefly bent upon avoiding actions which could benefit their rivals within the Coalition itself. In spite of Sybel, who, perhaps understandably enough for a Prussian historian, insisted that Prussia was primarily concerned with the defense of a just monarchical order against the wicked Jacobins and entertained no petty territorial ambitions,[21] the fact remains that the paramount aim of Prussia's foreign policy lay in avoiding as many obligations as possible of the St. Petersburg Convention while holding to its "advantages." In the words of a historian with less at stake than Sybel: "How to avoid continuing the war after the close of the present year, how to thwart the Bavarian Exchange . . . while still keeping up the appearance of favoring it, how to reduce to the minimum the 'additional advantages' stipulated for Austria in the Convention"— those were subjects for maturest deliberation at the Prussian ministry.[22]

Thus when the fall of Mayence and Valenciennes in the summer of 1793 offered the golden opportunity to mount a decisive attack on the French armies and make a speedy march toward Paris, a clever Italian, Lucchesini, in the service of the Prussian court as its envoy at Vienna, confessed that his government would surely object to any serious diminution of the power of

France for fear of upsetting the general balance of power in Europe.[23] It was perfectly understandable, given such consideration, that when Conde and Valenciennes fell to the Austrian armies of Coburg in July 1793, the Prussians should have refused to join their forces with the Austro-English troops. As a result, Coburg, without the necessary reinforcement from the Prussian ally, was forced to waste his army in the northeast where the French had few or no forces stationed. The strategic opportunity for a speedy march to the heart of France was deliberately wasted for diplomatic reasons. Meanwhile the Prussians, who under Brunswick succeeded in seizing Mayence on July 23 and subsequently blocking Landau, came to a peculiarly deliberate halt in order to avoid actions that might benefit only Austria. Austria, on her part, decided to concentrate her forces on the slow reduction of various towns and the French barrier fortresses in Flanders, precisely because of the previous British-Austrian understanding that Austria should acquire territorial compensations in French Flanders in return for the renunciation of the Bavarian Exchange Plan. England sent out small contingents, which, together with Hessian mercenary forces, were under the Duke of York's command, mainly for the conquest of Dunkirk, her long-cherished entry port to the continent, while refusing to take part in a joint attack on the interior of France which alone could have brought the war to a speedy and decisive conclusion.[24] All in all, what the battle of Neerwinden seemed to promise in March turned out by fall to have been an illusion, while the crisis of the French Republic had been turned in the meantime into an energetic and historically decisive offensive against the conservative order of Europe.[25]

To get a view of the actual dissolution of the Coalition, we must return once again to the crucial St. Petersburg Convention, which seemed to change, as far as the Austrians were concerned, the whole international system of Europe. As Philip Cobenzle stammered incoherently, dumbfounded with surprise and despair on being presented with the Convention by Razumovski and Caesar who appeared successively at the Viennese State Chancellery on March 23, 1793, "the French Revolution [seemed to be] only child's play, compared with this event."[26]

The immediate outcome, as we saw, was the replacement of Cobenzle with Thugut, and a declaration at Antwerp that the war would be conducted for the express purpose of territorial conquests. Thus Lord Auckland confessed at the Antwerp conference that "England too contemplates a very considerable compensation for herself." The Prince of Orange then remarked that, since everybody else was looking for compensation, he too hoped that Holland would not be excluded from such a profitable feat.[27] As for the Prussians, an overriding priority was attached to lending the least possible cooperation to the acquisition of advantages by Austria, which under Thugut resumed the traditional posture of Prussia's eternal enemy.

As Haugwitz wrote, the Prussians felt that "if Austria can reconquer the Netherlands, all the better for the Emperor and for us; we wish it sincerely and shall not desert his cause—but we must not forget that it is not our business to lead the way."[28] Even Sybel wrote that "before the beginning of the French campaign, a feeling arose of the necessity of proceeding with the greatest caution, and of not stacking, for the advantage of Austria, all those forces, which might perhaps be needed on the following day to meet the encroachments of Austria on the Empire."[29] The most unmistakable statement of Prussia's attitude was provided in the May 15th *Note Verbale* of Count Lucchesini to Reuss, in which Prussia denied flatly the validity of Thugut's so-called *"principe de parité d'avantages et d'agrandissements."*[30] The Prussian ministry further stated that Count Haugwitz had never given any assent to such a principle. The fact was, according to the *Note,* that where Austria was *"partie principale et attaquée"* in the French war, Prussia was merely *"partie accessoire et auxiliaire."* The conclusion was that Austria should feel very grateful toward Prussia for having sought her indemnification in Poland instead of France, although the right existed for Prussia to indemnify herself in France also. If Austria considered herself entitled to an indemnification somewhere, such a possible right did not have the same validity as that of Prussia in Great Poland.

This was of course the exact opposite of Thugut's philosophy. What is more remarkable about it is the fact that Prussia apparently made no effort to persuade Austria to accede to the St. Petersburg Convention for the partition of Poland. This complacency on the part of the Prussians can be accounted for only by the fact that the Prussian ministry must have calculated that any quick accession of the Viennese court to the Partition Treaty would have the effect of binding Prussia to the continuation of the French war. In other words, the pretext for avoiding cooperation in Austria's acquisition of her indemnities would be removed, since the pretext depended solely on the moral ground of Austria's intransigence toward the St. Petersburg Convention. Therefore, to the delight of a historian with an eye for irony in history, Prussia was actually trying to prevent the Viennese chancellery from reversing Thugut's original refusal to accede quickly to the St. Petersburg Convention, because only such a refusal could deliver the court of Berlin from any possible obligation to carry on the war along with Austria.

Russia, on the other hand, wanted the Emperor's accession to the Convention for precisely the same reason that prompted Prussia to want to avoid it. Without it, the Russians feared, the Prussians would have a perfect excuse for retiring from the war against France. It was obviously in the interest of Russia to bind the hands of her immediate western neighbor in the French affair. Therefore, to appease Austria, inasmuch as it was impossible to benefit her at the further expense of Poland (or so the Russian court thought, anyway), the Russian Tzarina decided to bestow her generosity on the Emperor with other people's territories. Markov told Cobenzle:

> Flanders, Lorraine, Alsace offer you a vast field for acquisitions. The King of Prussia offers to consent to the secularization of some bishoprics in Germany: take advantage of that. England will not be at all averse to the acquisitions that you may wish to make at the expense of France; . . . by acceding to the Convention you will give us the right to speak firmly and to oblige Prussia to do likewise.[31]

Vienna, however, decided that the question of acceding to the Convention could and should wait. In the meantime, the

Viennese ministry was to engage in one of the favorite sports of classical diplomacy, namely map revision. De Mercy, for instance, proposed to Thugut what he called *"mon plan gigantesque d'une frontière pour nous."*[32] De Mercy's plan included all the land as far as the Meuse and Somme, that is, Alsace, Lorraine, Artois, and half of Picardy. Thugut was more cautious. Even though there seemed little likelihood that England would object to the de Mercy scheme, as she herself was engaged in the serious effort to convert French colonies into the properties of His Majesty, Thugut was only too well aware of the extremely contingent nature of such a "gigantic" plan. To ensure Austria's indemnification, not one but several possibilities would have to be kept open. Thugut, therefore, did not abandon the hope of picking a slice of Poland. It was necessary only to add Venice as another possibility, should the plan for indemnification at the expense of France prove impossible of consummation. The new plan, in brief, was to retain Belgium and pick up a "gigantic" prize in France, or, in case of failure in the former plan, to turn to Polish and Venetian territories for compensations to balance off the Prussian acquisitions in Great Poland.[33]

In the meantime, there appeared signs that Thugut's design with respect to the Polish partition might not be as altogether hopeless as it had once seemed. The Polish Diet now assembled at Grodno was making an unexpectedly vigorous resistance to the consummation of the St. Petersburg Convention. It was most opportune for Thugut to take advantage of what he must have regarded as an embarrassing position for the Tzarina in order to delay the final realization of the partition treaty, which would spell the end of his plans for Poland. On July 12, Thugut commenced his diplomatic offensive by instructing Louis Cobenzle at the Russian court to appeal to the Empress of Russia to postpone the partition of Polish territories until the war with France had come to a successful conclusion. On grounds of both prudence and expedience, Thugut counseled Catherine to consider the certain effects of the partition on the world, a partition which could be carried out only by the application of violent means in the face of the vigorous resistance now being put up by the Polish Diet.

Besides, the Russians would remain complete masters of the Polish situation regardless of the delay counseled, and such a delay would surely be the only available means of ensuring Prussia's continued cooperation in the crusade against revolutionary France.[34]

Unfortunately for Thugut, his dispatch to Cobenzle arrived only when the Diet at Grodno had already given in to virtually all the demands of Russia. Only the fulfillment of Prussia's ambitions remained to be held up. Cobenzle, therefore, took it to be his task to try to postpone the final settlement of the Prussian design on Poland. Prussia, on her part, warned through Ostermann that the King's patience could not be indefinitely tested and that the Austrians deceived only themselves in thinking that the postponement of the partition would in any way bind Prussia to the continuation of the French war. On the contrary, Cobenzle was told that the King would probably be obliged to resort to violent measures in order to realize his designs on Poland and such a course would naturally supply an excuse for withdrawing from the French war altogether. There seemed to be nothing more Austria could do. Russia, however, intervened. Markov assured Cobenzle that Catherine wished to delay the consummation of the Prussian ambitions with respect to Poland—and she was able to do so for more than a month.[35] The period of one month that was gained for further Austrian diplomatic maneuvers, however, was to bring not the realization of Viennese desires but the final death sentence of the Coalition.

Thugut began his maneuvers by sending Count Lehrbach to "amuse" the Prussians. Thugut's detailed instructions for Lehrbach's mission had rested in the first place on the assumption that the Prussian ministry was opposed to the Belgic-Bavarian Exchange Plan, Austria's renunciation of which, already confided to the British, had been deliberately kept secret from the Prussians. The second assumption was that the King of Prussia must have made definite promises to the princes of Zweibrücken, contrary to the stipulations of the St. Petersburg Convention, which committed Prussia to the support of the Bavarian Exchange Plan. Upon these assumptions, Thugut believed that he could catch the Prussians in a trap by pressing them for the fulfillment of the Bavarian Exchange Plan in the hope of then drawing them out of the dilemma at the price of further commitments toward Austria's acquisitions at the expense of France.[36] It goes without saying that the success of Lehrbach's mission depended on the condition that Austria's renunciation of the Bavarian Exchange Plan was unknown to the Prussians. It was an event, therefore, of major consequence to Thugut's plans when Lord Yarmouth, charged by his court to persuade the Prussian ministry to renounce the idea of withdrawing entirely from the French war, arrived at the headquarters of Frederick William on July 10. The skilled diplomacy of Count Lucchesini succeeded in leading Yarmouth to confess the secret promise made by the Emperor to renounce the Bavarian Exchange Plan.[37] The essential premise of Thugut's policy in sending Count Lehrbach to the Prussians had now entirely collapsed. The failure of the latter's mission was a foregone conclusion.

In the meantime, the Prussian ministry arrived at the following determinations. In case the Polish Diet at Grodno capitulated to Prussia's demands, the King should declare that he no longer demanded the Emperor's accession to the St. Petersburg Convention, and that he would be obliged for financial and other domestic reasons to withdraw his troops from the French war unless his allies should guarantee a further indemnity somewhere substantial enough to compensate for his financial obligations. If the Diet should prove intransigent to the end, on the other hand, a further condition should be added to the above that it was absolutely necessary for the King to suspend all actions against France in order to attend personally to his own interests in Poland. In sum, Prussia's policy was based upon the notion that only a deliberate prevention of Austria's accession to the St. Petersburg Convention could provide the sorely needed pretext for Prussia's withdrawal from the French war.

Thus, when Lehrbach made several attempts to convince Lucchesini, at his first conference with him at the village of Edenkoben on August 21, that the King could procure the Emperor's accession to the Convention only by agreeing to the principle of parity in all advantages and compensations, the cunning Italian diplomatist in the Prussian service must have felt that all was indeed well under control. What made the joke even worse for Austria was that, mindful of Thugut's instructions, Lehrbach brought to the conference the question of Bavaria, stating that only the King's cooperation could overcome the antipathy of the Zweibrücken princes toward the realization of the Bavarian Exchange Plan. Lucchesini, who knew from Lord Yarmouth's confession that Austria was already committed to the renunciation of the Exchange Plan because of the objection of Whitehall, politely asked Lehrbach whether the antipathy of the princes of Zweibrücken, who would be helpless without the support of the Hohenzollern King, was the only obstacle in the way of satisfying Austria's ambitions with respect to Bavaria. Was there nothing to be feared about the reactions of London? Count Lehrbach was caught completely unprepared. He saw no other way out except to admit that some opposition had been raised by Whitehall. Lucchesini then declared that it would have been very unfair to place the entire responsibility for the failure of the Bavarian Exchange Plan in the hands of the King. With this charge, well prepared in advance and delivered with effect, the conference ended for the day.[38] The following days were spent by each trying to "amuse" the other.

Then, all of a sudden, Lord Yarmouth decided to put a finishing touch to the blunder he had already committed. He communicated to Lucchesini that a secret convention had been signed in June between London and Vienna by which the latter renounced categorically the idea of the Belgic-Bavarian Exchange Plan. Today, historians do not believe in the actual existence of such a secret convention. Lucchesini, however, had no way of knowing that the British diplomat was quite the master of the fabrication of nonexistent treaties. In any case, it seemed to be clear to Lucchesini that "This transaction destroys all the obligations which the Convention of Petersburg imposed on the King with regard to Austria's indemnities. . . ."[39] It remained only for the Prussian ministry to declare so openly with the King's official endorsement.

The task of the Prussian ministry was made easier by the turn of events at Grodno. The Polish Diet agreed to the Prussian demands on such conditions as were calculated only to exasperate the Prussian ambitions without deterring them. The ministers at Berlin had no difficulty in persuading the King to suspend all actions against France and turn his army on the Rhine to the Polish territory to enforce his claims in person. With only a few inessential reservations troubling his royal conscience, Frederick William agreed to go personally to Poland and to endorse a written declaration which became virtually the death sentence of the First Coalition. The arguments of the Prussian Mémoire which was communicated to Thugut on September 24 were hardly surprising.

In the first place, it was declared that Austria's refusal to accede to the St. Petersburg Convention obliged the King to attend personally to his indemnities in Poland. The King could no longer cooperate in Austria's campaign to acquire indemnities in France, which would have to be carried out without Prussia's assistance. Second, the King no longer deemed the Emperor's accession to the Convention essential. Finally, for reasons of financial and other domestic obligations, the King would be prevented from continuing the French war for another year, unless the allies should provide him with sufficient means of doing so.[40] To England, Prussia declared that she could not participate in the third campaign without adequate subsidies from the allies.[41] Prussia was of course well aware of the fact that the territorial market in Europe had by now been greatly depleted. In any case, the demand for subsidies being declined, Frederick William ordered his army not to engage in any further serious undertakings. The collapse of the First Coalition was complete.

•   •   •

The Revolution survived. It did so not so much through its own strength as because of the weakness of the conservative Coalition against it. The remarkable and instructive thing about the failure of the Coalition is of course the dramatic disparity between its military superiority and its political impotence. What can account for this?

Heinrich von Sybel, whose Prussian sentiment has already been noted, attributed the failure of the Coalition to "Thugut's folly and dishonesty . . . Austria's shortsighted eagerness for gain . . . Russia's inconsiderate enmity to German interests."[42] To a more detached observer, Prussia's behavior also would have to be included. More important from a sociological point of view, the significant fact was that all the participants in the Coalition behaved strictly within the limits of the traditional balance-of-power system. True to their conservatism, the crowned heads of European states and their faithful ministers acted almost single-mindedly as if nothing had happened and nothing had been altered by the Revolution. By doing so they had unwittingly contributed not only to the survival of the Revolution itself but also to the destruction of the system which was the very framework for their action. Inflaming the revolutionary imagination with a threat of a collective counterrevolutionary crusade, the members of the Coalition were yet primarily concerned with anything but the destruction of the French Republic. The most significant event in their eyes was the partition of Poland, the ramifications of which seemed to be infinitely more crucial for the general balance of power in Europe than the rise of a democratic regime in France.

This of course should not be surprising. After all, they were authentic units of the balance-of-power system and their behavior was bound to be conditioned by the behavioral rules of the system of which they were part. If they entertained no transnational ideological aims, they were only being true to their very nature. Nothing would have been more remarkable than the coming together of Prussia and Austria to compose their traditional rivalries, which were deeply rooted in their geography and history, in a common effort to defeat France for ideological reasons. Russia's obsession with the Polish prize was as natural, given the system, as Prussia's reactive concern over the same Polish territory. The fact was that the behavioral rules of the classical balance-of-power system did not anticipate a revolutionary challenge to the system itself. It was, therefore, quite understandable if the conservative rulers persisted in their traditional prejudices and patterns of behavior even in the face of a revolutionary challenge, which nothing in their experience had prepared them to understand to begin with. The general failure to transcend petty jealousies and mount a concerted attack upon the Revolution was deeply rooted in the nature of the traditional balance-of-power system; success in doing so would have been extraordinary in any place or time characterized by a similar international system.

In more impersonal language, it can be argued that the international system of the eighteenth century lacked an adequate compensating mechanism to deal with revolutionary disturbances, that is, challenges at the level of the system itself. The behavioral norms of the system, to which the conservative players seem to have stuck with an almost obsessive single-mindedness even in a revolutionary period, did not allow for revolutionary circumstances under which one of the primary participants in the system would marshall all of its energy for the destruction of the system itself. Without a compensating mechanism to counteract revolutionary disturbances, the survival and stability of the eighteenth-century balance-of-power system depended on the voluntary acceptance of the system's behavioral norms by the participating actors. There was no conscious and deliberate effort to institutionalize the task of system-maintenance. To a great extent, the latter was left to accident for the good reason that during much of the period of its operation, the behavioral norms of the balance-of-power system were "internalized," that is, voluntarily accepted.

Such an international system is inherently unstable—vulnerable to system-destructive disturbances—because the phenomenon of "internalization" of behavioral norms can mean no more than that the participating actors, or powerful states, are in the hands of those whose more narrowly defined class interests, as distinguished from the interests of the states as such, coincide with prevailing international norms. In contrast, consider the case of a domestic political system. The stability of a political system is likewise a function of, among other things, the degree to which its behavioral norms are "internalized" by the participating units, the individual actors. The difference is that, despite Plato's image of complex psychological agents within the individual actor, the latter's internalization of societal values is a far simpler affair than a society's internalization of intersocietal norms. The degree of predictability, therefore, is inherently lower, other things being equal, in the case of an international actor's internalization of behavioral norms than in the case of an individual actor in a national system. For this reason, it is much more difficult to assume a relatively stable pattern of behavior in international relations than within a domestic political system. The actors in the former system are much more complex, and they can throw away their internalized values far more unpredictably than can an individual actor.

This inherent instability rooted in the very nature of participating units of any international system constitutes a paramount reason for institutionalizing a compensating mechanism to deal with revolutionary changes within such units. In other words, one of the essential requirements for international stability can be formulated in terms of including in the behavioral norms of the international system such rules as to alert the participating units to potential threats to the system itself. But the irony is that the moment such rules are imposed upon the international actors, the chances are that, by virtue of their ideological and potentially transnational character, they may tend to complicate the process of international relations which they are originally intended to stabilize. This, as we all are aware, is the dilemma of the "collective security" idea. As long as we cannot assume the preponderance of the prosystem over against the antisystem forces, any attempt to institutionalize an automatic reaction against a potentially revolutionary action may actually backfire, plunging the world into a disaster more catastrophic than the one from which the collective-security system was intended to save it.[43]

A creative effort to discover proper institutional means that would be ensured against backfiring should of course continue, but, at the moment, it is appropriate to reflect on the nature of statesmanship in a revolutionary age. One virtue of statesmanship of course is that it is flexible—never automatic. Statesmen can respond to the changes in their environment with greater flexibility and sensitivity than can institutional mechanisms. They can, in other words, transcend the rules of their own game and adapt themselves to a new situation by devising new rules to meet a novel contingency.

But such a creative response to an unprecedented contingency is actually rare. Limited by the inertia of the system to which he has been accustomed, an ordinary statesman is more likely to respond to a new challenge with the familiar tools of the old world. His perception is also likely to be conditioned by the habits formed under preceding conditions. In fact, his very success in the prerevolutionary world becomes the source of his limitation in a revolutionary situation, for his claim to power and authority in the old world rested by necessity on his commitment to the rules of the now-challenged system. He would not have been a successful statesman had he lacked that serene confidence in the validity of the institutions of the old world which characterized such men as Pitt, Thugut, and Frederick William. To expect such men to doubt the adequacy of their accustomed institutions—the balance-of-power system, in this case—is to misunderstand the nature of conservative statesmanship itself. The exasperating labyrinth of diplomatic intrigues and territorial compensations in which the conservative actors were blindly enmeshed in the face of France's revolutionary challenge was only a natural outcome of their instinctive conservatism in both domestic and international politics. For them to have seen what Burke saw would have required that appreciation of relativity of life which was naturally closed to their limited imagination. To their narrow and self-indulgent vision, the possibility of the collapse of the old order seemed altogether academic and theoretical—and they were not interested in theoretical issues.

Is a Burke, then, the answer to the dilemma of conservative statesmanship in a revolutionary age? Obviously the Coalition would have had a much better chance of defeating revolutionary France if it had followed Burke's advice. From the beginning, Burke's message was that the Revolution in France posed an unprecedented and revolutionary challenge to the stability of the old order in both domestic and international life of Europe. Consequently he had preached a counterrevolutionary crusade for the purpose of restoring the legitimate government of Louis XVI.

Two things make it difficult to accept Burke's analysis unreservedly. First, he was factually wrong about the state of the Revolution in France when he first pronounced his negative judgment
upon it. In 1790, the French Revolution was not as radical as he
believed. There was no concerted plan to challenge the entire system of European relations as Burke had imagined. On the contrary, we have seen that the deterioration of relations between
revolutionary France and the conservative states of Europe was a
result of many factors which were not deliberately planned at all.
If Burke was later proved right, it was at least partly because of the
unimaginative response of the conservative states and not because
of any deliberate strategy on the part of the French to impose
their new ideology on the rest of Europe. The international behavior of France in this early period was a product of France's
sense of insecurity on the one hand and the struggle for power
within France on the other, both aggravated by the policies of the
crowned heads, as we have seen.

Perhaps a more fundamental difficulty in accepting Burke's
prescription lies in what might be called at some risk the secular
trend of history. After all, the values ushered in by the French
Revolution have triumphed in the long run over the old order.
There is a sense in which the old order in France needed to be
replaced by a new one. As Pitt's vision was fixed by the limits of
the international system of balance of power, Burke's understanding of the French Revolution was definitely conditioned by his
analysis of and commitment to the British tradition of political
life. The issue therefore arises as to whether a policy of crushing
the Revolution through foreign military action, even if it should
have succeeded in the short run, was destined to be the best solution in the long run. If the rise of the new order in France was
somehow irresistible, was not the task of the conservative statesmen to accept the necessary change and try to minimize its violent
impact upon international life instead of attempting to deny the
need for change itself? Even if a Burkian coalition could have
crushed the Revolution in 1792 or later, it is reasonable to assume
the general development of European history would still have

seen the eventual triumph of democracy and liberalism. The way to stabilize international relations in a new environment is not to deny the newness of the environment either through words or violent means, but rather to accept it and try to incorporate it into the overall scheme of things.

Could the French Revolution have been contained without violent rupture of the international system? Of course nobody can answer such hypothetical questions of history with absolute certainty. On the other hand, to refuse to think about anything other than what has actually happened has the effect of assigning the quality of "inevitability" to historical facts. Insofar as it is not warranted to be absolutely certain about the "necessity" of historical causation, it is legitimate to conceive of possibilities other than facts. One strong possibility, as our analysis has revealed, is that the Second Revolution, which brought revolutionary France more aggressively upon Europe, would have been less likely to come about if the reaction of conservative Europe to the Revolution had been based on a more imaginative understanding of the revolutionary dynamic. Without pretending to absolute conviction, it is nevertheless possible to assert that the Revolution could conceivably have been incorporated into the international life of Europe without the quarter of a century of bloodshed on the scale required for the Revolution to destroy the old order in international relations, if the conservative statesmen of Europe had understood the nature of the French Revolution correctly and adapted their policies accordingly. The vision required for such reaction was conspicuous by its absence.

The result was that the Revolution survived and, defeating the first European Coalition against it, came to acquire the fatal quality—excessive self-confidence combined with a self-righteous sense of mission—which led the newly born French Republic to the self-imposed task of remaking not only France but the whole of Europe. The war begun partly out of insecurity and partly for domestic reasons was now transformed into an ideological struggle between the Revolution and the crowned heads of European states. The irony is that in this destruction of the old order in international relations, no small part was played by the conservatives themselves, but in the process they had no idea of what was being done to the very basis of their international life.

Notes

1. Feb. 5, 1790. *Parliamentary History,* Vol. XXVIII, pp. 353–367, printed in Alfred Cobban, ed., *The Debate on the French Revolution, 1789–1800* (London, 1960), p. 67.
2. Grenville to Auckland, June 19, 1792, in *Report on the Manuscripts of J. B. Fortescue, Esq.,* edited by Great Britain Historical Manuscripts Commission (London, 1892–1927), Vol. II, p. 281. Hereafter referred to as *Dropmore Papers.*
3. Grenville to Auckland, Nov. 6, 1792, *The Journal and Correspondence of William Auckland,* edited by the Bishop of Bath and Wells (London, 1861), Vol. II, pp. 464–467. Hereafter referred to as *Auckland Journal.*
4. Quoted by George Rud, *Revolutionary Europe, 1783–1815* (Cleveland and New York, 1964), p. 121.
5. J. H. Clapham, "Pitt's First Decade," in *The Cambridge History of British Foreign Policy,* Vol. I, Chap. I, p. 213.
6. *Archives parlementaires,* Vol. LIII, pp. 512–513.
7. *A Collection of State Papers Relative to the War Against France* (London, 1794–1799), Vol. I, p. 217.
8. Grenville to Auckland, Nov. 13, 1792, *Dropmore Papers,* Vol. II, p. 339.
9. See Chapter VI.
10. Burke to Grenville, Aug. 8, 1792, *Dropmore Papers,* Vol. II, pp. 463–466.
11. Grenville to Auckland, Nov. 27, 1792, *Dropmore Papers,* Vol. II, p. 344. Also Grenville to Auckland, December 4, 1792, *ibid.,* p. 351.
12. Holland was already an ally when the war broke out.
13. The seizure of Toulon is made famous of course by the first appearance of Napoleon Bonaparte, then a young artillery officer.
14. G. F. de Martens, *Traités conclus par la Russie,* Vol. II, pp. 228–235.
15. Robert Howard Lord, *The Second Partition of Poland, A Study in Diplomatic History* (Cambridge, Mass., 1915), p. 398.
16. *Ibid.,* p. 401. See also J. Holland Rose, *William Pitt and the Great War* (London, 1911), p. 122.
17. For the entire text of the Memorial see A. R. von Vivenot (Vols. I and II) and H. von Zeissberg (Vols. III–V), *Quellen zur Geschichte der deutschen Kaiserpolitik Oesterreichs während der französischen Revolutionskriege, 1790–1801* (Wien, 1873–1890), Vol. II, pp. 798–801. Hereafter referred to as Vivenot and Zeissberg, *Quellen.*
18. Von Thugut to Reusse and Louis Cobenzle, April 14, 1793, *ibid.,* Vol. III, pp. 11–13.

19. Von Thugut to de Mercy, April 4, 1793, *ibid.*, pp. 24 ff.
20. De Mercy to von Thugut, Sept. 15, 1793, quoted by Heinrich von Sybel, *op. cit.*, Vol. III, p. 490.
21. *Ibid.*, pp. 135 ff. See also Vol. II, pp. 461–465.
22. Robert Howard Lord, *op. cit.*, pp. 415 ff.
23. Quoted by J. Holland Rose, in *The Cambridge History of British Foreign Policy*, Vol. I, p. 240. See also Eden to Grenville, Vienna, August 31, 1793, *ibid.*, Appendix B, p. 553: "H.M. would object to any serious diminution of the power of France as upsetting the balance of Europe."
24. For these strategic "blunders" see Albert Sorel, *op. cit.*, Vol. III, pp. 489–499; Heinrich von Sybel, *op. cit.*, Vol. III, pp. 135–143; A. Fugier, *Histoire des relations internationales*, Vol. IV; *La Révolution française et l'empire Napoléonienne* (Paris, 1954), pp. 84–86.
25 For the battle of Neervinden, see A. Chuquet, *La Trahison de Dumouriez* (Paris, 1891), 2nd series of *Les Guerres*, pp. 96–104.
26. Quoted by Robert Howard Lord, *op. cit.*, pp. 403–404.
27. Quoted by Heinrich von Sybel, *op. cit.*, Vol. II, p. 464.
28. Quoted by Heinrich von Sybel, *ibid.*, p. 451.
29. *Ibid.*
30. For the entire text of the *Note Verbale*, see Vivenot and Zeissberg, *Quellen*, Vol. III, pp. 63–67.
31. Robert Howard Lord, *op. cit.*, p. 420.
32. De Mercy to von Thugut, June 15, 1793, Vivenot and Zeissberg, *Quellen*, Vol. III, pp. 112–113.
33. Von Thugut to Stahremberg, August 13, 1793, *ibid.*, pp. 184 ff.
34. Von Thugut to Louis Cobenzle, July 12, 1793, *ibid.*, pp. 141–145. 141–145.
35. Louis Cobenzle to von Thugut, July 30 and August 2, 1793, *ibid.*, pp. 156–158, 160–161.
36. "Punctation," August 3, 1793, *ibid.*, pp. 163–169.
37. Robert Howard Lord, *op. cit.*, p. 432.
38. Lehrbach's report, August 21, 1793, Vivenot and Zeissberg, *Quellen*, Vol. II, pp. 198 ff.
39. Quoted by Robert Howard Lord, *op. cit.*, p. 436.
40. Vivenot and Zeissberg, *Quellen*, Vol. III, pp. 290–295.
41. *Dropmore Papers*, Vol. II, p. 441.
42. Heinrich von Sybel, *op. cit.*, Vol. III, p. 149.
43. For a critical but sympathetic treatment of the collective security system, see Inis L. Claude, Jr., *Power and International Relations* (New York, 1962), pp. 150–204.

V

The Robespierre Regime:
Moderate Aims and Revolutionary Means

Revolution in the aims of France's international relations was clearly the work of the Girondin party. Revolution in the means of pursuing international action, however, awaited Robespierre, who had replaced the Girondins after a fierce struggle for power that took place throughout the fall and winter of 1792 and was finally decided in favor of the Mountain only after Dumouriez had defected to the Austrians on April 5, 1793. Beaten at Neerwinden and subsequently driven out of the Netherlands, Dumouriez tried at first to persuade his army to march on the Convention at Paris in a plot to disperse the Jacobins and restore the monarchy with Louis XVII on the throne. When the army refused to follow this highly improbable plan for a counterrevolutionary coup, Dumouriez decided that there was no more future for him in France, and as a result went over to the Austrian side. Understandably enough, this treason by the original architect of the war on the House of Austria was blamed on the Girondins.[1]

Defection of Dumouriez, however, was no more than an immediate occasion for the fall of the Girondin-dominated regime. As the National Convention, which agreed on April 6 to set up a special Committee of Public Safety without a single Girondin among its nine members, was mostly made up of the moderate party, the Plain (often contemptuously called the Marsh or the Belly for its opportunism), the triumph of the Mountain under Robespierre over the Gironde had deeper causes than the mere blunder of Dumouriez. There seem to have been basically three reasons for the fall of the Gironde. They are, first, the tactical mistakes committed by the Girondin politicians themselves, second, the economic crisis, and, finally, the circumstances of the war.

Tactically, the attitude (shown by the leading Girondin figures) toward the September massacres and the trial of Louis XVI did nothing to win popular approval, a new element in politics that was becoming increasingly decisive in any contest for power. First, the Gironde blamed Parisian clubs and sections for the September massacres, even going so far as to persuade the Convention to disband the "revolutionary" Commune. The liquidation of the Commune was not against the interest of the Mountain either, since the perpetuation of the Commune would have meant an independent center of power away from the Convention where, after all, the Mountain belonged. But the important point is that the Mountain was not identified in the public mind with the policy of repudiating the Commune, a symbol of uncompromising revolutionism, whereas the Gironde definitely was so identified. Secondly, on the trial of Louis XVI, the Girondins were hopelessly divided. Some among them went so far as to demand that the King's life should be spared, while others suggested a referendum. If united, the Gironde might have been able to save the King's life, but divided as they were, the only effect of their various demands was to earn the nickname, *"les appelants,"* an expression of contempt on the part of sans-culottes. The King of course was sentenced to death, and once again the Mountain managed to project itself as the consistent champion of uncompromising revolutionism, while the credentials of the Gironde as a party of the Revolution were being seriously questioned in the public mind.

The economic crisis tended to have a similar effect. As the value of the assignat fell rapidly and prices consequently soared, lower classes began to demand government control of prices. Again failing to understand the political importance of the popular demand, the Gironde objected to all forms of governmental interference with economic life. This cleavage between the Gironde and the Parisian sans-culottes regarding the need for controlling economic life has led some historians to see a sharp class

conflict between the bourgeoisie and the proletariat, the former
including the Mountain as well as the Gironde.[2] Be that as it may,
the net effect on the immediate struggle was once again to reinforce
the image of the Mountain as the champion of the cause of the
Revolution, while the motives of the Gironde were becoming
increasingly suspect.

Popular suspicion of the Gironde still might not have had a
decisive impact on the outcome of the power struggle had it not
been for the fact that the circumstances of a foreign war naturally
tended to link any suspect with possible treason to the fatherland.
Robespierre, a brilliant and ruthless tactician, did not hesitate to
exploit this situation to picture his opponents as a party not only
opposed to the Revolution but also betraying France in an hour
of gravest danger. Thus, when the Section Halle au Blé circulated
a proposed petition to the Convention demanding action against
hoarders, speculators, and monopolists, including some Brissotins,
Robespierre defended the petition, not on account of any economic necessity but to defeat "treason" against the fatherland.
Casting suspicion on Dumouriez's failure to pursue and destroy
the Prussians after Valmy,[3] Robespierre told the Convention that
the Brissotins really disapproved of the annexation of Savoy and
Belgium, a sure sign of their betrayal of the Revolution itself.
Conveniently forgetting that it was he, Robespierre, and not the
Brissotins who had cautioned France against too reckless adventurism in foreign policy, the new leader of the Mountain revealed
that Brissot did not really want "the revolution of Europe" and
was now anxious to make peace with the foreign enemies in order
to restore a monarchy in the Orleans line.[4]

At the height of his newly found passion for international revolution, Robespierre demanded the death penalty for anyone
who dared to suggest compromise with the foreign enemy. Danton
managed to soften the proposal before it finally was enacted into a
Decree of April 13, 1793.[5] Repeating the now familiar pledge not
to interfere with the government of other powers if they in turn
recognized "the sovereignty, independence, indivisibility, and
unity of the Republic founded on liberty and equality," the decree promised the death penalty for anyone favoring compromise

with an enemy of the Republic. The significance of the "no interference" pledge was of course nil, since recognition of the "indivisibility" of the Republic would have meant acquiescence in the
annexations—which the monarchs of Europe considered only
temporary at most. The decree is important because it shows that
Robespierre's change of posture from that of an opponent of the
war in the earlier period to one of its new champions was based
on a sound tactical instinct. In identifying himself openly with aggressive internationalism, Robespierre correctly understood that
he was stealing away from the Girondins the one sure basis of
their contact with the popular revolutionary tide.

The victory of the Mountain was therefore a result of two
most fundamental factors merging into one, namely, the war and
the Revolution. Opposition to one came to mean automatically
disapproval of the other. To be sure, this equation between domestic and international revolutions was to a great extent the
work of the Girondins themselves. Their final failure, as was
pointed out earlier, lay in refusing or being unable—perhaps for
reasons of fundamental class interest—to follow to its logical conclusion the popular momentum they themselves had helped to
generate. Robespierre, a more ruthless tactician, did not hesitate to
ride the popular tide if doing so meant power for him and defeat
for his opponents.

Robespierre's calculations were finally confirmed on June 2
when several thousand armed sans-culottes, organized by the Commune and the Jacobin "machine," surrounded the Tuileries,
where the Convention met, with the help of the National Guard
and demanded the arrest of 22 Girondin deputies. The August of
1792 repeated itself. The Convention once again yielded to the
demand of the crowd. To the cries of *"Vive la Montagne"* and *"A
bas les traîtres,"* the Mountain took over the leadership of the
Convention.

In July, the Convention formed a new Committee of Public
Safety composed of twelve Mountain members, including Robespierre who would become the committee's front and most powerful leader, and the remarkable Lazare Carnot who was to
demonstrate a military genius by reversing the fortunes of the Re-

public once again. Thus a new phase had begun in the short history of the Revolution, and the regime headed by Robespierre began to put its distinct stamp on the conduct of the war.

Interestingly enough, though, the Robespierre regime began its career by adopting a rather moderate posture with regard to many revolutionary aims. Although the Convention provided for the first time in the Constitution of June 1793, which was subsequently ratified by the primary assemblies throughout the country as the Constitution of the Year I, a system of government both republican and democratic, the regime under Robespierre was in no hurry to put it into effect. After all, it was not surprising if Robespierre felt his first need was for more power and not less. There was internal insurrection at Lyons, Marseille, and Bordeaux where original federalist agitation was increased by the bourgeois' anger over the expulsion of the Girondins, while the revolt of the Vendée peasants in support of their "tyrants," that is, priests and landlords, had yet to be put down completely. It was during this early period of the Robespierre regime that Marat was mysteriously assassinated in his bathtub. Most crucial of all of course was what seemed to be the imminent march of the Allied forces into the heart of Paris. In this critical summer of 1793, Robespierre found himself turning against two forces which more than anything else were responsible for bringing him into power, namely, popular democratic revolutionism and revolutionary internationalism.

First, on the domestic side, Robespierre began by repudiating popular democracy in favor of a representative system. Sobered by the possession of power, this arch-Jacobin did not hesitate to define "democracy" as "a state in which the sovereign people, guided by laws of its own making, does for itself what it can do well and by its delegates what it cannot."[6] Anyone who dared to oppose this definition of democracy and demanded dissolution of the Convention in the name of the Constitution of the Year I was called an "ultrarevolutionary," which, according to the new orthodoxy, was the same thing as a counterrevolutionary. The new Revolutionary Government was obviously determined to show where power lay and to keep it there for some time.

More significantly, from our point of view, the new Revolutionary Government headed by Robespierre had also turned against revolutionary internationalism. Ignoring the fact that his main weapon against Brissot had been the charge that the latter betrayed the policy of revolutionary expansionism, Robespierre now adopted the more moderate posture of Danton by defining the war aims in more concrete and realistic terms. This new spirit of moderation in foreign policy, which even Brissot did not dare to advocate openly for fear of appearing a traitor to the Revolution, found its official expression in the Convention's Decree of September 15, 1793. It declared that the generals of the Republic should renounce thenceforth the "philanthropic idea . . . of trying to make foreign nations appreciate the price and advantages of liberty." Instead, it was announced, they "shall conduct themselves toward the enemies of France in the same manner as the Allied powers conduct themselves toward it: They shall observe, toward countries and individuals conquered by French arms, the ordinary laws of war."[7]

The causes for the change of mood must have been complex, but according to Robespierre himself, the chief reason was that France could now afford to be less aggressive because her survival was assured. France had proved "invincible" and the tyrants were inevitably coming to the end of their conspiracy to bring down the Republic. Besides, Robespierre was convinced that "the power of reason" was sufficient "to propagate the principles of our glorious Revolution." If not, no matter, since "the French are not afflicted with a mania for rendering any nation happy and free despite itself." Indeed, it was Robespierre's view that "all the Kings could have vegetated or died on their bloody thrones had they known to respect the independence of the French people."[8]

The foreign policy of Robespierre's regime had therefore the following three basic principles.

First, despite the Jacobin rhetoric, the Revolutionary Government had explicitly renounced the messianic aims of revolutionary expansionism. No more conquests would be attempted in the name of spreading liberty and equality.

Second, the basis for foreign relations thenceforth would be

the legal status of the French Republic as a sovereign and independent state, and no longer the social principles of the Revolution. Having renounced the universalistic claims of an earlier
phase, the Republic declared itself to be ready for peaceful coexistence with conservative states, so long as its territorial integrity
and political independence were not violated.

Finally, the Convention vouchsafed that it "will treat with
none of the foreign agents and ministers who do not have a positive status with respect to the French Republic."[9] This was of
course a logical corollary of the second principle which signaled
France's return or desire to return to the world of positive legal
norms. More important than this was the fact that the Revolutionary Government under Robespierre was making a genuine attempt to end the tide of revolutionary internationalism, a
movement that was now regarded as a form of conspiracy against
the solid achievement of the Revolution. As Palmer put it most
vividly, Robespierre was really convinced of

> a vast foreign conspiracy, composed of all kinds of "ultras,"
> both the popular and international kind, preaching the *rév-
> olution à outrance*, insatiable activists, enemies of all govern-
> ment and all religion, working in collusion with old Bris-
> sotins, "moderates" and accomplices of Dumouriez, rein-
> forced by super-Terrorists who feared that the Revolutionary
> Government would repudiate them, joined by grafters and
> common cheats who feared exposure, driven frantically
> onward by the machinations of true counterrevolutionaries,
> royalist agents, clandestine clergy, and foreign spies who
> wished to throw the Republic into chaos so that monarchy
> and aristocracy could be restored.[10]

It is small wonder then that the chief aims of Robespierre's foreign policy were mainly nationalistic and "realistic." Like Stalin
in our time, Robespierre felt that his first task was to defend the
realm physically and consolidate the Revolution in one country.

If this were all that could be said about the foreign policy of
the Revolutionary Government, it might be concluded that the

only thing needed to minimize the impact of a revolution on international relations is a Robespierre, or, more precisely, stabilization of the decision-making process in the political system of a country that has experienced the revolution. But we know this is not the case. Indeed the more violent consequences of the impact of the Revolution on international relations of the time were to become known only in a later development.

Actually the truth of the matter is that while redefining the aims of foreign policy in rather moderate terms, the Revolutionary Government had instituted for the first time revolutionary means for achieving those nationalistic aims.[11] Robespierre found it necessary, to protect the achievement of the Revolution, to mobilize the resources of the state to a far greater extent than the crowned "tyrants" had ever dreamed of in their pursuits of military glory. In doing so, he had significantly affected the pattern of international relations.

The mobilization of the state took mainly two forms, military and economic. First, the military mobilization was declared in the famous *levée en masse* on August 23, 1793. This was in response to a series of military defeats suffered during the month of July, when the Prussians had recovered Mainz and the British seized their long-coveted prize, Toulon. The decree itself limited military conscription to "unmarried men between the ages of eighteen and twenty-five."[12] More important than mere conscription, however, was the idea that all the citizens were obliged to aid the state. Twenty years after Rousseau dreamed of a citizen army imbued with *"l'amour de la patrie et de la liberté,"* something of the same spirit was actually born under the government of Robespierre.[13]

Of course not everything can be left to enthusiasm alone. More than a million men with diverse social backgrounds had to be forged into a functioning army. Discipline had to be combined with patriotism. Naturally, suspected officers were purged and new ones created. When the Representatives on Mission had finally completed their task of eliminating the elements suspected of treason, Carnot, the genius who succeeded in integrating "volunteers" with "regulars" to build a new army, formulated a new criterion of loyalty. "A defeat is not a crime," said Carnot, "when everything has been done to merit a victory. We do not judge men by events but by their efforts and their courage. We care only that they do not lose hope for the salvation of *la Patrie*."[14] The new citizen army of the Republic was truly founded on the new spirit of a romantic age, elevating the ethics of intention above those of consequence.

The significance of this new citizen army cannot be exaggerated. Its creation made it possible to employ systematically brigades and divisions arrayed in long, thin lines. As the old system of cordons and sieges was due, in part at least, to the mercenary character of the troops, the new tactical innovation resulted from the numerical superiority made possible by popular conscription and the confidence the officers could have in the loyalty of troops recruited from the patriotic citizens. Ironically enough, it was through the achievement of the Jacobin regime under Robespierre that Napoleon was able to challenge the rest of Europe. Consciously or not, the creation of a national army could not but add to the increasing dynamism of violent contacts between nation-states.

The initial pressure for the economic mobilization came from the sans-culottes, who demanded governmental control of soaring prices. As we have seen, unlike the Girondists, who had refused to accede to this popular demand, the Montagnard had no scruples about intervening in the economic life of the country. On September 23, 1793, a general "maximum" was set up on all important commodity prices and wages throughout France.

The Revolutionary Government also instituted a system of government requisition for military purposes, and swiftly extended its control to consumer life by creating the *pain d'égalité*, a coarse bread made from mixed flours, while forbidding the baking and sale of fine white bread and *pâtisserie*. Foreign trade was regulated by the Committee on Provisions, while the Committee of Public Safety directly controlled productive sectors of the economy.[15] The Committee of Public Safety also had the power to try anyone suspected of refusing to comply with the economic regulations of the government and to seize their property for suitable distribution among the more worthy. The basic idea of the economic mobilization was a very simple one, namely, that every citizen should work for *la patrie,* from shoemakers who were required to produce two pairs of shoes per journeyman every ten days to scientists engaged in the arms industry and research.

Did all this, however, mean some form of socialism? The fact that the original impetus came from the sans-culottes, combined with the nature of the subsequent Thermidorean reaction, led some scholars to the impression that Robespierre was indeed a precursor of socialism. On the other hand, the Revolutionary Government never attacked private property as such. By confiscating and redistributing the property of those suspected of treason to the Republic, the Revolutionary Government was in effect endorsing the notion that "the property of patriots is sacred."[16] To be sure, this is not a Lockian view—but then it is hardly a Marxian idea either. It is essentially a nationalist idea.

The economic control of the Revolutionary Government was basically a war measure. The wage earners and sans-culottes reaped most of the advantages, yet the essential historical significance of the so-called "economic terror" is not that it was a foretaste of economic egalitarianism of the future but rather that for the first time in modern history a conception of economic mobilization for a state purpose went beyond the familiar routine of tax collection. The gap between Babeuf and Robespierre is a real one. If the former stands for a certain social gospel, the latter's significance lies primarily in innovations in the technique of governmental control. In sum, the Revolutionary Government's unique contribution to the process of the old international system's destruction was in the realization of a thoroughly modern and democratic idea that in time of war the entire nation is to be mobilized for unreserved participation in the war effort. Understandably enough, the achievement of the Revolutionary Government in the field of economic and military mobilization had assured the survival of the Republic against the Allied powers. The survival of Robespierre and his regime, however, was another matter. The military successes brought about by Robespierre's own determined efforts also made it possible for France to dispense with his

stern and tyrannical services without collapsing before its conservative enemies.

The Allied powers too seem to have contributed substantially
to making the military success of the Republic possible. As we
have seen, unable to resolve conflicts among their separate war
aims, the armies of the conservative powers were more or less consciously drifting into a state of immobility. The Republic lost no
occasion to take advantage of such a golden opportunity to defeat
the invasion. The new national army under Generals Jourdan,
Hoche, and Pichegru began to reverse the military fortune in the
fall and by December of 1793 both Worms and Spier fell into
French hands. December was also memorable for the recovery of
Toulon from the British, an accomplishment made possible by
the dazzling genius of a young artillery captain, Bonaparte. The
height of the military success came on June 26 in the following
year (1794) in the critical Battle of Fleurus. The French army,
now employing the more flexible brigades and divisions, forced
the Duke of Coburg to evacuate Belgium. A month later, on July
27, Robespierre too was forced out of power.

●   ●   ●

It will be recalled that in outlining the structure of international relations in the prerevolutionary period, it was tentatively
suggested that the limited nature of interstate conflicts was probably due to the limited nature of resources available to the rulers
of the ancient regimes as well as their conscious aims. This relationship between the stakes involved in interstate conflicts and the
means available to the main actors in an international system
becomes even more clear when we take a little longer look at history. The French Revolution, or more precisely the Revolutionary Government under Robespierre, which injected into Western
history a new concept of national mobilization for state action,
marks the beginning of what might loosely be called the era of
total war.

The full meaning of the Revolution in the means of state action would not be known, to be sure, until a century later, in
1914. The First World War, begun without any conscious design

for total conflict, nevertheless became such by virtue of the inescapable requirement for national mobilization, as Raymond Aron
has so brilliantly shown.[17] The difficulty in recognizing a historical
trend, however, is that history rarely moves in a linear fashion.
There was bound to be a time gap between the Robespierre
regime's revolution in the means of state action and the full
realization of its implications. After all, the restoration of the
balance-of-power system in the postrevolutionary period was a
quite successful operation. The peacemakers of 1815, if they
achieved anything, had succeeded at least in postponing the full
effect of the Revolution upon European history. What they could
never accomplish was to obliterate the connection between the
means of state action and the stakes in interstate conflicts. Once
the former had been revolutionized, it was inevitable that the
latter would be affected as a result. This, in short, is the most
fundamental contribution of the Revolutionary Government to
the process of destroying the classical balance-of-power system. Not
through conscious design for the ideological revolution of Europe,
but by mobilizing the entire French nation regardless of its social
divisions for the paramount objective of national defense, the Robespierre regime ushered in a new era of nationalism and total
war. Henceforth, the rulers of nation-states would no longer hesitate, as the rulers of monarchical states did, to impose taxes on
nobility and recruit freely from commoners. What is more, the
ruled would serve not just for the sake of money but more often
for the love of their fatherland.

Nationalism is of course not the sole agent for the revolution
in the means of state action. The resources available to the rulers
depend to a decisive extent on the level of technological development. However, the role of technology is both more obvious, particularly in this age of nuclear weapons, and less significant than
the role of ideology in influencing the stakes of interstate conflicts.
It is interesting, for example, that Carnot and his colleagues, who
were engineers by profession, did not bring about any significant
innovation in the weaponry of the ancient regime, while succeeding so spectacularly in the creation of a new national army. The
truth is that, while technology is always decisive in shaping the na-

ture of international relations, its own development is inextricably intertwined with the web of social and economic relations, and, furthermore, its role in the evolution of international relations depends to a very great extent on men's attitude toward it and their capacity to control its power. Tentatively at least, it can be suggested as a plausible hypothesis that the accelerating pace of technological development in modern history may be related to the newly felt requirement in the age of nationalism for an ever increasing effectiveness in state action. As the stakes grow higher in modern interstate conflicts, so grows the need for more efficient technology.

It is not being asserted here, as Marx tried to show, for instance, that technological development depends entirely on economic or political change. In all probability, the relationship is reciprocal, each influencing the other, but from the point of view of analyzing the process of the destruction of the classical balance-of-power system, the role of ideology is undoubtedly more interesting than that of technology. As we have seen, during the French Revolution there was no fundamental innovation in weapons technology as significant as the innovations in the ideological realm. If the latter brought about the collapse of the classical balance-of-power system through a revolution in the means of state action, as this chapter has tried to show, then technology was not an equally decisive factor in this development. The more decisive role, it is argued here, was played by ideology.

Ideology, however, contributed to the collapse of the classical balance-of-power system not so much by altering the nature of consciously sought objectives in international relations as by making available new and more dynamic means of action for the rulers of nation-states. All too often when the role of ideology in the field of international relations is discussed, both those who inflate and those who minimize the significance of ideological factors tend to define ideology solely as a set of objectives and aims. What is neglected is that ideology, by helping to define and determine the domestic structure of the actors themselves, also influences the nature of means available for state action.

This is certainly true of the Revolutionary Government's

case. If the regime under Robespierre was no shining example of a nonaggressive state with modest aims defined in terms of physical survival, all the evidence nevertheless points to the "realistic" and nonsupranational character of the objectives sought by the Revolutionary Government. If the Robespierre regime contributed to the collapse of the classical balance-of-power system, it was not because it consciously sought to do so but because, regardless of its conscious aims and objectives, in its actions it could only be true to its own nature, namely, by seeking to fulfill its aims through completely unorthodox and revolutionary means of national mobilization in both economic and military spheres. By doing so, it undermined one of the major foundations on which the limited nature of traditional interstate relations depended.

The role of ideology is therefore a complex one. First, most obviously, it sets up new goals, as we have seen in the case of the Girondin expansionism. Then it also partly influences the nature of the means available for pursuing those goals, as the case of the Revolutionary Government illustrates vividly. Finally, these two interact with each other, the clearest example of which occurs when an ideologically conservative state tries to meet the challenge of a revolutionary power. Even if ideology did nothing more than inject new goals into international relations, the task of meeting the challenge of a revolutionary power would be difficult enough. But what complicates the task even more is the fact that, since a revolutionary power is likely to pursue its goals through a more thorough and consistent mobilization of the entire nation-state, the only way a conservative power can meet the challenge successfully is often by revolutionizing its own mode of action. Of course the dilemma here is that by revolutionizing its own means of action, a conservative power inevitably runs the risk of betraying the substance of its own ideological commitment. This, in essence, has been the predicament of conservative powers in the age of rising nationalism.

The same predicament, however, constitutes an advantage for a revolutionary power, since the latter does not limit its means of action to those sanctioned by the inherited system of rights and obligations. Indeed, it is in the very nature of a revolutionary power that its mode of action is free from traditional inhibitions which bind more or less effectively the hands of all conservative rulers. No more dramatic illustration exists of this strategic advantage of a revolutionary power than the flexibility shown in Napoleon's mode of action. Throwing aside all the accepted norms and doctrines governing the behavior of states to each other, the inheritor of the Revolution was free to innovate brilliantly in his method of struggling against other powers.

This, however, is getting ahead of our story. For the moment, it is sufficient to observe that the revolution in the means of state action, which was the work of the Robespierre regime, was fundamentally due to the newly rising democratic and nationalistic ideology, and gave to France a strategic advantage of incalculable value. To be sure, since a revolutionary power is always in the minority in the early stage of revolutionary transformation of the international system, conservative powers alone have the option of an alliance based on the common interest in defeating the revolutionary challenge in its inception. As we have seen in the last chapter, however, such a mode of action requires of conservative rulers imaginative insight into the nature of a revolutionary challenge and the capacity to overcome ordinary tensions and rivalries of a traditional international system. Lacking those qualities, the conservative rulers of the First Coalition did nothing more than make an empty gesture, while their real ambitions and energies were concentrated elsewhere. It is small wonder that the French Republic stood to gain all the strategic advantages of being a revolutionary power while suffering from none of its disadvantages. Neither is it surprising that France, combining the revolution in aims as effected by the Girondin regime and the revolution in means as achieved by the Revolutionary Government, was able to destroy the international system of the ancient regime single-handedly. How such a combination came about is the concern of the next chapter.

Notes

1. H. A. Goetz-Bernstein, *op. cit.*, pp. 384 ff.

2. See, for instance, George Rudé, *The Crowd in the French Revolution* (Oxford, 1959): Albert Soboul, *Les Sans-culottes parisiens de l'An II: Mouvement populaire et gouvernement révolutionnaire, 2 junin 1793 à 9 thermidor An II* (Paris, 1958).

3. That Valmy was a near miracle and no orthodox general would have pursued the enemy to destroy its troops after a battle was of course conveniently forgotten by Robespierre, and perhaps by other Jacobins as well.

4. Robespierre, *Oeuvres*, Vol. IX: *Discours*, IV (Paris, 1958), pp. 376–416.

5. For Danton's speech, see *Discours de Danton*, edited by A. Fribourg (Paris, 1910), pp. 394–400. For the decree, see *Moniteur*, Vol. XVI, p. 143.

6. C. Vellay, ed., *Discours et rapports de Robespierre* (Paris, 1908), quoted by R. R. Palmer, *The Age of Democratic Revolution*, Vol. II, p. 115.

7. *Archives parlementaires*, Vol. 74, p. 231.

8. *Histoire parlementaire*, Vol. XXX, pp. 224 ff., 317.

9. F. A. Aulard, ed., *Recueil des actes du comité de salut public avec la correspondance officielle des représentants en mission et le registre du conseil executif provisoire* (Paris, 1889–1951), Vol. VII, p. 29, quoted by Sydney Biro, *op. cit.*, Vol. I, p. 193.

10. R. R. Palmer, *The Age of the Democratic Revolution*, Vol. II, p. 120.

11. Taking a larger view, Godechot sees "means of the expansion" over a longer span of time than I do. He deals with *"la propagande spontanée"* which includes theatre and arts as well as press, and *"l'action du gouvernement"* under which he discusses the new national army as well as diplomacy. Jacques Godechot, *La Grande Nation: L'Expansion révolutionnaire de la France dans le monde de 1789 à 1799* (Paris, 1965), Vol. I, pp. 99 ff.

12. *Histoire parlementaire*, Vol. XXVIII, pp. 469–471.

13. J.-J. Rousseau, "Considerations sur le gouvernement de Pologne et sur sa réformation projetée," in *Oeuvres complètes de J.-J. Rousseau,* edited by V. D. Musset-Pathay (Paris, 1823), Vol. V, Chap. XII, "Système militaire," p. 344.

14. M. Dumolin, *Précis d'histoire militaire* (Paris, 1901–1912), Vol. I, p. 206.

15. For economic mobilization, see Crane Brinton, *op. cit.*, pp. 130–137; George Lefebvre, *The French Revolution*, Vol. II, pp. 100–110. For an older view, see Albert Mathiez, *La vie chère et le mouvement social sours la Terreur* (Paris, 1927).

16. Saint-Just, "8 Ventoe, an II," *Moniteur*, Vol. XIX, p. 68, quoted by Crane Brinton, *op. cit.*, p. 136.

17. Raymond Aron, *The Century of Total War* (New York, 1954).

VI

From the Thermidoreans to the Directory:
Resurgence of Expansionism

There are very few settled questions in history. The Thermidorean reaction is not one of them. From the beginning, the fall of Robespierre has elicited two contending interpretations. Some historians, like the late Albert Mathiez, insist that the Thermidorean reaction was a genuine case of social-class conflict.[1] Others, like Proffessor R. R. Palmer, look upon the 9th Thermidor as another episode in the constant struggle among personalities for power.[2] Truth, as in most such debatable issues, may actually lie partly on both sides for, if it was the personal struggle that brought about, in the most immediate sense, the fall of Robespierre, the subsequent dismantling of the Revolutionary Government was certainly an indication of a shift of power from one social class to another. Despite Barère, who declared on the 10th Thermidor that the event of the previous day amounted only to "a slight commotion which left the government untouched," the energies released by the fall of Robespierre were bound to affect the fate of Thermidoreans themselves. There was no question that the sans-culottes were deprived of their power. The Maximum was repealed and private property, regardless of whether it belonged to patriots or not, once again became sacred.

If power slipped out of the hands of the sans-culottes, it devolved understandably enough upon those who made the 9th Thermidor possible in the first place, namely the center known as the Plain. The majority of the Convention, which had always been in the middle, was so assured of the security of the French

nation by the military successes of the Robespierre regime that
when Robespierre's personal enemies among the Montagnards demanded his fall, most men at the center did not feel it necessary
to retain his services any longer. By relying on the consent of the
Plain for the removal of Robespierre, of course, the Thermidoreans were unwittingly making themselves the captives of the center. This they did not realize at the moment, which was, after all,
the moment of their personal triumph. In any case, the remnants
of the Mountain would constitute an opposition only on the left,
as the Gironde and royalists returned to form the right. The new
men from the Plain were now sitting in their somewhat unexpected positions of power. Henceforth, everything would depend
on the center's ability to play the left and the right against each
other. Whether they could succeed where the men of 1789 had
failed remained of course quite a problem.

In the meantime, the dismantling of the Revolutionary Government led to a new chaos in the war economy, while increasing
desertion and the government's failure to call up new reserves resulted in a substantial reduction of troops. Despite these factors,
the momentum generated earlier by the victory of Fleurus was
strong enough to sustain the forces of the Republic through the
fall and winter of 1794. The immobility of the Allies, which, as
we have seen, was a result of their traditional rivalries and tensions, also contributed to making possible the military success of
Thermidorean France. First, the victors of Fleurus, now called
the Army of the Sambre-et-Meuse, easily captured the Ruhr and
forced the Austrians across the Rhine once again. The Army of
the North under Pichegru seized Maestricht and, by January of
1795, went on to occupy Holland, forcing the Prince of Orange-
Nassau to flee to England.

The French occupation of Holland gave new life to the
Dutch Patriot movement, which had been temporarily crushed
through the combined force of British diplomacy and the Prussian army. Reviving the indigenous revolutionary movement, the
French proclaimed within a month of their occupation the estab-
lishment of the Batavian Republic, which was to become the first
of the so-called "Sister Republics of France." The difficulty with

the creation of a Sister Republic in Holland, however, was that it raised the uncomfortable question of whether or not a similar treatment should be accorded to the other peoples and territories conquered by the Republican soldiers. There was of course no controversy about Nice and Savoy, which were now unquestionably attached to the Republic, indivisible and independent. But what about Belgium and Rhineland? Should they be annexed or left alone? Should they be urged to become Sister Republics? The Thermidoreans were hopelessly divided at first. For instance, about the Rhineland left bank, there were some who, like Merlin of Thionville, were opposed to the idea of annexation since in their view the key to general peace was in retaining only the "former frontiers" of France.[3] On the other side of the debate were those who advocated annexation of the Rhineland left bank for one reason or another. Reubell, for instance, was an Alsatian by birth and naturally wanted to protect his native province from future German attack, while Sieyès wanted to annex the left bank in order that France could dictate the remapping of Germany while checking Russia's western advances.[4] Between these two extremes were found those who could not make up their minds. Both Merlin of Douai and Boissy d'Anglais hesitated to commit themselves to either side. The interesting thing, however, about the whole debate was that neither side resorted to ideological talk. The annexationists, as well as those opposed to them, were arguing in "realist" terms of national security and concrete advantages. There was no revival of Girondist or Hébertist revolutionary internationalism.

If the Rhineland issue remained unsettled, the problem of Belgium did not. Persuaded by Carnot's "realistic" arguments for annexation, the Convention voted on October 1, 1795, to make Belgium part of the French Republic. Again, the significant thing was that annexation of Belgium was justified in terms of presumably "realistic" advantages to France rather than revolutionary rhetoric about liberating the oppressed peoples.[5] There was no doubt that the Thermidoreans, true to their nature, were set against reviving the fervently messianic foreign policy of the Girondist period, which even Robespierre did not find wise to carry

on. The emergent mood was unquestionably one of "realism."
The new men of the center were more concerned with the preser-
vation of the acquisitions already made by the French army than
liberation of Europe from its crowned tyrants. Let the tyrants
rule over their proper subjects. As long as they were prepared to
accept the survival of the Republic as an accomplished fact, the
new rulers of France were also prepared to conduct themselves in
the traditional spirit of pursuing negotiable aims and concrete advantages.

It was this spirit of emergent "realism" in Thermidorean
France that made it possible for France to negotiate successfully a
number of peace treaties in the spring and summer of 1795.

First, following the relatively unimportant peace with Tus-
cany, which was concluded on February 19, 1795, France signed
with Prussia the Treaty of Basel on April 5, 1795.[6] Motivations
were thoroughly traditional on both sides. France wanted above
all to weaken Austria by coming to terms with Prussia, whereas
the latter, without the English subsidy which had been cut off in
the fall of 1794, saw no reason to pursue the war with France any
longer. Besides, it seemed imperative for Prussia to get out of the
war if she was to protect her interests in the East, since Russia and
Austria were clearly coming to terms with each other for a final
partition of Poland. Understandably, Prussia wanted to keep her
hands free for such a contingency.[7] In the treaty itself, cessation of
hostilities was agreed upon between France and Prussia on the
condition that France should occupy the left bank of the Rhineland until general peace was concluded with the Empire, while
northern Germany was to be neutralized. Actually though, Prussia had consented by a secret clause to the absolute cession of the
left bank to France, which in return promised to compensate
Prussia through secularization of ecclesiastical territory on the
right bank. There could be no clearer instance of a typical classical diplomatic deal entailing territorial compensations. The
French Republic, only three hundred days ago proclaiming the
liberation of the whole of mankind as its unalterable and supreme
task, now did not hesitate to enter into an arrangement that gave

no thought to the factor of nationality, let alone political liberty and other revolutionary goals.

Peace with Spain was concluded in June of the same year on the basis of similarly secular and sober considerations. The death of the ten-year-old dauphin, Louis XVIII, having removed the last obstacle, Barthélemy for France and Yriarte for Spain were finally able to agree to a treaty. France, eager to neutralize Spain, agreed to evacuate all occupied Spanish territory except the island of Santo Domingo, which was ceded to France. Spain, feeling the military superiority of France, wanted above all else to get out of the war from which she could not expect to gain anything.

France followed her treaties with Prussia and Spain by concluding peace with Saxony, Hanover, and Hesse-Cassel, leaving in the war only England on the sea and Austria and Portugal, the latter the "perpetual ally" of England, on the continent. Even against these remaining powers, there was no more revolutionary rhetoric. Having acted as any other ancient regime would have done in setting up the Hohenzollern against the Hapsburg by concluding the Treaty of Basel, France resumed in its struggle with England the familiar traditional contest for colonial and commercial supremacy, while conducting the war with Austria mainly for territorial advantages in the new policy of *divide et impera*. In any case, even if France wanted peace with Austria, the latter with its Imperial domain was less eager for it since Vienna saw no reason to worry about the Russian designs on Poland as Prussia clearly did.

The crucial question at this point then is this: Why did international relations fail to reinstate the classical balance-of-power system? What prevented Europe from restoring its traditional international principle of limited ends and limited stakes? Everything seemed to point in that direction. France had repudiated the Republic of Virtue and was now reconciled to a world of more or less sinful men whose business it was to make life possible and not to purify it. Revolution of Europe seemed to be quietly forgotten. The crisis of revolutionary and ideological expansionism seemed to belong in history. Nevertheless, the traditional balance-of-power system would not be restored until the peacemakers of Vienna consciously strove to reconstruct it. Indeed the crisis in the international life of Europe that was witnessed in the years 1792 to 1795 was nothing compared with the violent explosion that would engulf all of Europe in the following years. Why?

The question is all the more compelling because the government of the Directory, which inherited the power of the middle class from the Convention dominated by the Thermidoreans, not only continued the Thermidorean policy of pursuing moderate and negotiable aims instead of trying to liberate the oppressed peoples, but also actively sought to come to terms with the two remaining powers in the war, Austria and England. To be sure, the efforts of the Directory showed no consistent eagerness for peace. The men who governed France from 1795 until the 18th Brumaire in 1799 were diverse enough in personal background and political convictions to make it virtually impossible to achieve a unified policy on the problems of peace and war with Europe. But to charge the Directory, as Sorel did, with complete and conscious insincerity in its various negotiations for peace is to misunderstand the nature of governmental process in the French political system of the time.[8] Decision-making was extremely diffused and erratic, and as a result the Directory's foreign policies never achieved a clear-cut consistency. The Directory was characterized not so much by lack of sincerity as by weakness.

In any case, the Directory made a number of approaches to Austria and England. First, toward Austria the Republic made a series of diplomatic overtures from the so-called "Poteratz mission," and Carnot's secret attempt through Zwanziger, to an approach made through the Queen of Naples.[9] In all these attempts at negotiating peace, the Directory showed a willingness to satisfy the Hapsburgs by offering Austria such compensations as Bavaria (for the possession of which Vienna had already acquired the consent of Catherine II), Salzburg, the Upper Palatinate, Berchtesgaden, or some other Italian territory which the Holy Roman Empire might desire.

In the case of England, it seems to have been the fluctuations of English policy that were largely responsible for the failure of peace negotiations between the government of King George III and that of the French Republic. England first approached France when the former's prime minister, Pitt, sensing the return of normality in France, ordered Wickham to contact Barthélemy, who had negotiated the treaty of Basel, at Berne, in order to sound out French attitudes. This overture, however, came to nothing, probably, as Sorel argued, owing to lack of sincerity on the part of the English. Wickham insisted on addressing the French ambassador merely as "Monsieur" and referring to the French Republic only as "France."[10]

Later, in October of 1796, Lord Malmesbury was sent to Paris on another mission. Again England did not seem to be very eager for peace, since Grenville's instructions to Malmesbury required as a condition for peace with France that the Belgic Provinces should be restored to Austria, a condition that the Directory would not and could not accept under the circumstances. The interesting thing about the question of Belgium is that Delacroix, French minister of foreign affairs, justified the French possession of Belgium on the ground that it was necessary to restore the European equilibrium, which he contended was destroyed by the Polish partitions and the English conquests on the sea. In any case, it was no secret that neither King George III nor his foreign minister, Lord Grenville, had much wanted the peace negotiations to succeed. Both hoped to see the end of the regicide regime.

Additional financial burdens, however, forced Pitt to try once more to negotiate peace with the Directory. Negotiations were conducted at Lille in the summer of 1797 between Malmesbury of England and three members of the Directory, including Maret, the ex-prisoner of Austria and future Duke of Bassano.[11] This last figure was almost synonymous with opportunism, and, conspiring with Talleyrand who was no less adept at looking after his own interests, Maret had entered into all sorts of shady dealings with Malmesbury such as selling false French documents for speculation on the stock market. Such individual opportunism would have done no harm were it not for its effect on Malmesbury, who gained the impression that, because of their "practical" bent, the French negotiators could swing the entire Directory in the same direction. More specifically, Malmesbury believed that Carnot and Barthélemy would be able to take care of the more stubborn Reubell, who, as we have seen, was unyielding on the point of retaining the conquered territories, particularly the left bank of the Rhineland and the Netherlands. This was a false impression. The Directory took a position somewhere between that of Reubell and the more flexible Maret and insisted on keeping its "natural frontiers," while consenting to relinquish Holland on the condition that England should secede to Spain and Holland her maritime and colonial conquests in order to restore the balance of power. Finally these negotiations came to a dead end, for England was unalterably opposed to giving up her conquests on the seas.

It may be argued of course that, since the Directory insisted on retaining its "natural frontiers," the failure to realize peace at this point was due to the expansionist policy of the Republic. But that France's position was not unreasonable under the circumstances was borne out by the fact that Gouverneur Morris, England's own good friend, gave similar advice to Grenville in his letter of October 5, 1796.[12] What is important really is not so much whom we should blame for the failure of negotiations as recognition of the fact that the Directory, despite its inconsistencies and fluctuations in policy, was far from being determined, as the Gironde regime had been, to upset the entire European system of interstate relations. It was not worried about a unified European counterrevolutionary attack nor planning to liberate the oppressed peoples from their crowned tyrants. If the Directory was anxious to retain its "natural frontiers," it was a relatively conservative posture, given the fact that they had already been under the French rule for some time. In fact, as the expansionism of Napoleonic France would demonstrate later, the concept of "natural frontiers" was a restrictive idea, depending on the circumstances and one's point of reference.

Despite all these facts which point to the return of "realism" in the thinking of the French rulers, one hesitates to blame the failure of peace negotiations on the conservative powers. The reason for this is very simple, for the fact is that the military initiative in the years 1797 and 1798 was in the hands of the French and not of the conservative states. The Armies of the Republic were literally pouring out in all directions, as if by force of gravitation, setting up on their way so-called "Sister Republics" with their comic Roman names. In Italy, for instance, the conquering French forces created the Cisalpine Republic on July 9, 1797, followed by the Ligurian Republic in Genoa, and the Roman Republic in February of 1798. Switzerland, except Geneva which was directly annexed to France, became the Helvetic Republic by April of 1798.

Finally the height of these military successes came when the Republican troops, under the command of the brilliant young general Napoleon, landed in Egypt in July, 1798. Although the ultimate aim of the expedition was doomed to frustration, the Egyptian expedition caused the conservative powers to come together by the autumn of 1798 in the Second Coalition against France. Once again, as in 1792, Europe was bipolarized into warring camps, one the French Republic, and the other an alliance composed of England, Austria, Russia, Portugal, and Turkey. This time, however, there was no cause for alarm for the French as there was in 1792. On the contrary, for the French, the war of the Second Coalition was an adventure in expansionism, whereas the war of the First Coalition had been, at least in its origins, a defensive action.

How then can we account for this upsurge of expansionism, particularly after the return of "realism" in post-Thermidorean France? To anyone familiar with the history of the period, the answer is obvious: It was to Napoleon more than anything else that the new expansionism was due. To be sure, the Directory too, on Carnot's advice, had launched its own campaign against the Austrian Empire. But the Directory's effort to weaken the House of Hapsburg was intended to create a balance between Prussia and Austria so that France could play the game of *divide et impera*. It was Bonaparte's spectacularly successful Italian campaign that injected a hitherto unprecedented dynamism into the foreign policy of France and began to spread the Revolution beyond the limits set by "Nature," the latter being for him a restraining condition, and not a conception for expansion.

Lacking any philosophical sympathy, Bonaparte was nevertheless carrying out Buonarrotti's grand design for "perpetual peace" by setting up Sister Republics. And it was Napoleon's fertile romantic imagination combined with the revolutionary instrument of the national army that finally completed the process of destroying the classical balance-of-power system. Henceforth, he had decided, peace would be guaranteed not by equilibrium but through the hegemony of one power, France. To be sure, the peace obtained at Leoben on April 18, 1797, was a work of Napoleon, who had signed it without consulting the Directory at Paris, but this peace, which was converted into the Treaty of Campo Formio on October 17, was regarded as no more than a tactical truce by both France and Austria. As a matter of fact, Napoleon signed the peace merely to buy time so that France could concentrate all her energies on bringing England down. "That done," exclaimed Napoleon, "Europe will be at our feet."[13] This dream was of course never completely realized. But France under Napoleon had succeeded at least in ruining the old system of interstate relations—and that needs to be explained.

●   ●   ●

To a social scientist, the role of a hero in history is always an unsettling one. Most of the time, he can more or less submerge individuals under the wave of social movement, but when the role played by an individual is as conspicuous as that of Napoleon, it is not so easy to speak in sociological terms alone.[14] For working social scientists, however, the problem of assessing the role of a hero in history can be at least temporarily "solved" by avoiding the problem at its general level and instead concentrating on a concrete issue. What can we say then about Napoleon? There are several things that can be said about his role.

In the first place, the phenomenon of Napoleon was a confirmation of Robespierre's fears. As early as January 1792, Robespierre, then opposed to the war, argued that one of the greatest dangers of a foreign war, if it were victorious, would be the possible rise of military generals as political dictators.[15] The origins of Napoleon's rise are quite clear. They were derived from the circumstances of the war itself, as the origins of the Second Revolution were also due to the circumstances of the war. For that matter, the dictatorship of Robespierre himself was not unrelated to the war either. In any case, the relationship between the war and the domestic politics is most striking.

Second, the fact that Napoleon played a decisive role in breaking up the traditional system of interstate relations does not imply an accidental theory of history. His role can be explained as a function of certain impersonal factors. His personality certainly was important, but, without resorting to the Hegelian language of the so-called "world-historical individual," there is no denying the fact that his personality became an instrument of certain social forces which were not entirely his own making. More specifically, his rise to power was due basically to the particular nature of the bourgeois regime which governed or tried to govern France between 1795 and 1799. Historically, his name cannot be separated from "Fructidor" and "Floréal."

The regime under which Napoleon's rise was made possible was of course the product of the Thermidorean reaction, which meant not the end of the Revolution as some historians have imagined but rather the return to the principles of 1789. It was a repudiation of the Republic of Virtue, and not the Revolution as such. Essentially, therefore, the post-Thermidorean regime was inevitably caught between two extremes, left and right. True to its nature, it was equally opposed to the radical democracy demanded by the Jacobins and sans-culottes on the one hand and the royalist restoration dreamed of by the reactionaries and émigrés on the other. The Directory, however, failed to create its own basis of support by alienating the moderate bourgeois elements through fluctuating and largely unworkable policies. Under such circumstances, the Directory could maintain its power only by playing the left and the right against each other. The trouble with this strategy was that the artificial equilibrium between right and left could be maintained only if the Directory could guarantee enough power of its own to defeat potentially violent challenges from either side. Lacking any substantial social support, the Directory, as we know, could turn only to the army in extreme crises. This is precisely what the Directory did when through the *coup d'état* of Fructidor of the Year V (September 1797), it defeated the right. Again in the *coup d'état* of Floréal of the Year VI (May 1798), the Directory relied upon the Republican Army to defeat the left.[16] On both occasions, the loser was the Constitution of the Year III (1795); the winner was the army and its shining example of republican victory, General Bonaparte, who would of course complete the process in 1799 through the *coup d'état* of Brumaire, putting an end to the facade of power held by the now moribund Directory.

More specifically, the turning point was Fructidor (September 4, 1797), in which the more conservatively oriented members of the Directory, Barthélemy and Carnot, were eliminated. They were replaced by more republican deputies, François de Neufchâteau and Merlin de Douai, the second of whom was largely responsible for breaking the negotiations with England at Lille and probably allowed Napoleon to sign a temporary tactical truce with Austria. Fructidor, as might be expected, was a defensive action against the right, who were suspected of planning a coup of their own against the Republic. The important thing, however, was that in carrying out their coup, the Directory had to rely on Bonaparte, who sent one of his generals, Augereau, to provide the actual power. Augereau arrested Pichegru and Barthélemy, while Carnot escaped. Henceforth, from Fructidor, the Directory was to be definitely under Napoleon's control—and as we have seen, the foreign policy of France took a new turn. Displaying the direction of its future, the new "Second" Directory did not hesitate to let the Dutch democrats carry out their *coup d'état* against the federalists and declare a more radical Republic in January of 1798. As real power was drifting to the army and Bonaparte, the stability of European life was going to pieces. The Revolution of 1789, begun without international pretensions, was finally succeeding in wrecking the inherited classical system of interstate relations. That the rise of Napoleon, which was largely due to the nature of the regime within France as well as to the circumstances of the war, had a decisive impact on the final stage of dissolution of the traditional interstate system seems to me beyond dispute.

There are other theories, however. First, there is the economic explanation, according to which the French expansionist policy was a deliberate attempt by the Directory to exploit certain natural resources of the Austrian Empire, such as Bavaria's salt.[17] It is further argued that the Directory could have come to terms with Prussia for reasons of commercial trade. The difficulty with this economic explanation is that there is really no tangible evidence to support it. There is no proof, for instance, that the Directory had consciously followed the policy of weakening the Empire for the express purpose of exploiting the latter's natural resources. The whole argument is no more than mere conjecture and therefore cannot be accepted as a full explanation of the upsurge of expansionism in French foreign policy in the years we are dealing with. A more plausible, though hardly more convincing, explanation in terms of economic motivation would be that it was probably the need to supply its troops with provisions which were not available in sufficient quantities within France alone that drove the Directory to the policy of letting its armies advance indiscriminately in all directions. The fact is that the Directory did actually allow its armies to conquer and live off new territories, particularly in 1795. Again, the difficulty with this interpretation is that there exists no evidence that the exploitation of conquered territories was indeed the conscious and primary purpose in the minds of decision-makers.

Another view of the expansionist foreign policy of the Directory is propounded most persuasively by Albert Sorel, who sees an unbroken continuity in French foreign policy from the Ancient Regime through the Revolution to the Directory. He asserts that the Directory was never really serious about general European peace, but in fact was very much bent upon carrying on the age-old contest between the Hapsburg dynasty and the French Bourbons. Like most grand historical generalizations, Sorel's thesis is not without some element of truth. There was certainly something like historical continuity in the tensions and rivalries between France and Austria. But to maintain that no fundamental change took place in the relations among states in the age of the Revolution is really to adopt a view of history so sweeping as to be completely indiscriminate, even with regard to quite meaningful changes. Sorel's view may be accurate as far as it goes, but by leaving out so many significant and crucial elements, it is ultimately blinding.

Finally, there is the more sociologically inclined view of Godechot and Palmer. As has already been pointed out, both historians maintain that the spread of the Revolution was due more to the general revolutionary situation throughout Europe than to the deliberate work of the French revolutionaries. This position is certainly worth further study, which lies outside the scope of this essay. The Godechot-Palmer argument, though quite innocently presented by them, would ultimately lead us to the question of a secular trend in historical change. Not merely the French Revolution, but the entire process of modernization of Europe is at stake here. If one takes this sociological approach, one must view international relations within the inclusive context of what might loosely be called "total history." The changes taking place in international relations become then part of a far wider historical movement.

It seems to me that the Godechot-Palmer thesis is essentially valid, if it is not overstretched. Generally speaking, it is quite true that the French Revolution was not an isolated incident confined to France alone. There was definitely something like a revolutionary unrest throughout Europe at that time, signaling the eventual death of the *ancien régime*. No doubt the spread of the Revolution was at least partly due to this pervasive revolutionary situation. To stop at this point, however, and explain everything else as a result of this vast secular change in European history is as indiscriminate and blinding as Sorel's insistence on an unbroken continuity in the history of international relations. Both explanations are only partly valid and not particularly helpful. Although the expansionism of the French Republic was undoubtedly due to the general revolutionary situation, the fact still remains that France pursued a more expansionist and unsettling course of action after Fructidor than before. This fact cannot be explained by a sweeping generalization across the entire revolutionary age. From our analytic point of view, the unambiguous and specific changes in the process of destabilization are far more interesting than the somewhat metaphysical idea that everything happening in an age may be related to one single unifying theme. Also, when we come down to explaining the specific and concrete changes taking place in the course of the destruction of the traditional interstate system, the phenomenon of Napoleon presents a more rewarding object of interest and inquiry than the pervasive revolutionary spirit of the age.

What then does "Napoleon" mean?

First, it means once again that the connection between domestic politics and international relations is a highly critical one. There is a constant process of mutual interaction between these two spheres of public life. If Napoleon's rise can be attributed to the circumstances of the war (international relations), his ultimate seizure of power was made possible by the peculiar social position of the regime that he helped maintain and finally replaced (domestic politics). The impact of his seizure of power, too, was both international and domestic. He was forced to maintain his power only through the dynamism of his foreign and military policy; his international adventurism would have been unthinkable without the material accomplishment of the Revolution, namely the nation-state and the democratic idea of national mobilization for state action. Without going into the Napoleonic period, which lies outside the scope of this essay, it is not difficult to see that any attempt to construct a chain of causes for the final collapse of the classical balance-of-power system would have to include as critical factors both the domestic and international aspects of the phenomenon that Napoleon represents.

Second, "Napoleon" means a synthesis of Gironde and Robespierre, that is, a combination of the former's expansionism in aims of foreign policy and the latter's accomplishment in revolutionary means of state action. Seen in this light, Napoleon becomes anything but "accidental." His personality may have played, as indeed it must have, a quite decisive role in fusing these elements. Insofar as his personal contribution was based on those elements that were

integral to the Revolution, however, the resurgence of expansionism in French foreign policy can be explained as a phenomenon
deeply rooted in the entire revolutionary process itself. It was no
mere accident that the Directory failed to restore peace and stability to European relations. France, even under a "moderate" regime, was bound by that time to be driven by revolutionary forces
that were already the inescapable heritage of the Revolution. The
popular vision of revolutionary mission and the nationalist idea of
total state mobilization—these were the very elements that were im-
planted into the French body politic by the experiences of the Revolution itself and unscrupulously exploited by Napoleon. In
other words, Napoleon did not create the materials that made it
possible for him to challenge the European system. He merely exploited them.

Finally, in pondering upon the meaning of Napoleon, one
cannot escape a nagging suspicion: If Napoleon was very much an
integral part of the Revolution and his accomplishment in international life, negative as it was, can be viewed only as one of the
necessary effects of the Revolution, the dilemma of the conservative powers was ultimately insoluble, for to minimize the destructive impact of the Revolution on international relations would
have necessarily entailed the negation of the Revolution as such
from the beginning. After all, was Burke really right? Insofar as
Napoleon's destruction of the European system was inevitably
bound up with the Revolution, both in its domestic and international aspects, Burke's advice to destroy the Revolution and restore
the *ancien régime* would seem to have been the only workable
"solution" for the maintenance of international stability.

Such a Burkian solution, however, poses two difficulties.
First, it is based on the unexamined assumption that the restoration of the *ancien régime* would have been possible only if the
conservative statesmen had had the right vision and acted accordingly. The fact is that not only did conservative statesmen lack the
required imagination and determination, but even if those qualities had been present, it is extremely doubtful that the conditions
that led to the Revolution in France would have allowed the restoration of the *ancien régime* through foreign intervention. The

later developments, including the failure of the July monarchy, would suggest rather the contrary conclusion, namely that, whatever its effect on international relations, the Revolution in one form or another was quite inescapable. Given this assumption, Burke's exhortation to undo the Revolution completely sounds rather unrealistic.

The second difficulty, however, may be more serious. Since the restoration of the *ancien régime* would have been no simple matter, to say the least, a concerted European attempt to accomplish it might have brought about precisely those destabilizing and catastrophic consequences in the relations between France and the conservative states which it was presumably Burke's intention to avoid. In other words, a Burkian solution would most likely have been self-defeating.

Then were the conservatives in an insoluble dilemma? The answer to this question would be affirmative only if we deal with the Revolution as a single event. To do so is greatly misleading. If we look at the revolutionary process in terms of its specific phases rather than in terms of its overall impact, it is not too difficult to discern possibilities of viable conservative action in minimizing the destructive impact of the Revolution on international relations. It is the purpose of the following, concluding chapter to do precisely this by recapitulating the basic findings of this study and suggesting possible general hypotheses based upon those concrete findings.

Notes

1. Albert Mathiez, *La Réaction thermidoreanne* (Paris, 1929).
2. R. R. Palmer, "Fifty Years of the Committee of Public Safety," *Journal of Modern History*, Vol. XIII, p. 1941.
3. *Correspondance de Merlin de Thionville*, Vol. II, p. 185, cited by Sydney Biro, *op. cit.*, Vol. I, pp. 368–369.
4. Raymond Guyot, *Le Directoire et la paix de l'Europe des traités de Bale à la Deuxiemme Coalition, 1795–1799* (Paris, 1911), pp. 118–119.
5. *Moniteur*, Vol. XXVI, p. 121.
6. For a more detailed description of negotiations leading up to the signing of the treaty, see Sydney Biro, *op. cit.*, Vol. I, pp. 312–352; also R. Guyot, *op. cit.*

7. As for the English subsidy, the irony is that actually on April 9, four days after the signing of the treaty of Basel, George III, who was emotionally attached to Prussia, proposed to Lord Grenville that the subsidy for the Prussian Army be renewed. *Dropmore Papers,* Vol. III, p. 50.

8. Albert Sorel, *op. cit.,* Vol. V, Chap. 1.

9. See Sydney Biro, *op. cit.,* Vol. II, pp. 514–521, 551–556, 680–689, 704–729; also Raymond Guyot, *op. cit.,* pp. 205–207.

10. Raymond Guyot, *op. cit.,* pp. 153–155. *British Annual Register,* 1796, p. 421. For the general description of the negotiations between England and France, see *Cambridge History of British Foreign Policy,* Vol. I, pp. 261–281.

11. *Diaries and Correspondence of James Harris, First Earle of Malmesbury,* edited by the Third Earl of Malmesbury (London, 1844–1845), Vol. III, pp. 376–406.

12. *Dropmore Papers,* Vol. III, p. 258.

13. *Correspondance de Napoléon Ier* (Paris, 1858–1870), Vol. III, p. 520.

14. For an interesting analysis of the problem of the hero in history, see Sidney Hook, *The Hero in History: A Study in Limitation and Possibility* (Boston, 1955).

15. *Histoire parlementaire,* Vol. XIII, p. 153.

16. R. R. Palmer, *The Age of the Democratic Revolution,* Vol. II, pp. 231–260.

17. Sydney S. Biro, *op. cit.,* Vol. II, pp. 960–966.

VII

Conclusions:
Toward a Theory of International Stability

International relations have been rightly defined in terms of their anarchic milieu, but the fact that nation-states interact with each other in the so-called "state of nature" does not mean that international relations are uniformly disorderly or interstate conflicts always equally deadly and destructive. Anarchy, after all, is not the same thing as the absence of order, although the latter is often the consequence of the former. Given the anarchic condition, international relations still exhibit varying degrees of violence and stability. It is as if some periods in the history of international relations were more "anarchic" than others, much as some animals are said to be more "equal" than others. The essential condition of anarchy does not, in other words, obliterate the very real and significant differences in the degree of stability and violence between one period of international relations and another. It is precisely for this reason that a monistic theory of international relations, whatever form it takes, is bound to be somewhat inadequate, since it stresses unity and continuity rather than diversity of patterns and trends and changes in the history of international relations.

If some periods in history are characterized by a greater stability than others, the question naturally arises: What accounts for it? What are the conditions, the absence of which tends to plunge nation-states into a world of unrestrained competition and unlimited conflict? To answer this question—or more precisely, as a preliminary step in an effort to discover such an answer

—we have undertaken in this book to analyze a process of destabilization of international relations. It is hoped, if our findings
are supported by further empirical studies, that it will be possible
to isolate those variables that form the enabling foundations of
stable patterns of interstate relations. But as I indicated earlier,
this study is only a preliminary step to performing the task of isolating the conditions of international stability. The more immediate concern throughout this study has been to discover the factors
that contributed to the breakdown of a relatively stable pattern of
international relations, in this case the classical balance of power,
and analyze the ways in which those factors worked destructively
upon the existing international system. In brief, this book is a
study of the breakdown of an international system.

How then does an international system break down? Although the question is far from being original, surprisingly little
effort has been made to answer it explicitly. In fact, it is doubtful
if traditional scholarship has ever raised the question at such an
explicit and general level. Studies of the eventual dissolution of
the Vienna settlement, the collapse of the Bismarkian system, and
the failure of the peace of Versailles—all such studies tend to stop
short of pursuing the question of international destabilization to
its general and theoretical level. It is only quite recently that
scholars have begun to concern themselves seriously with the possibility of formulating general theories of international systems
and their breakdown. Two most explicit efforts to achieve this
objective are Morton Kaplan's highly original work, *System and
Process in International Politics,* and Richard Rosecrance's more
recent study, *Action and Reaction in World Politics.*[1]

Kaplan began by defining international relations in terms of
systems of action and postulating six distinct international systems. Each of these systems is characterized by a corresponding set
of "essential rules," which presumably describe the characteristic
behavior of the actors in a given system. Thus, for instance, the
"balance-of-power" system was discussed in terms of a set of six
behavioral rules which were said to be in "equilibrium" with
each other. Having thus specified the essential behavioral rules of
the "balance-of-power" system, Kaplan went on to suggest the fol-

lowing "conditions which may make unstable the balance-of-power system":

> the existence of an essential national actor who does not play according to the rules of the game; the existence of a national actor whose essential national rules are oriented toward the establishment of some form of supranational political organization; failures in informational inputs into the decision-making systems of national actors or personality inputs which are deviant in terms of the essential rules; capability changes which are characterized by positive feedback; difficulties in applying the other rules when applying either the rule to increase capabilities or the rule to restore defeated actors or inconsistencies between the rules and pressing national needs; and difficulties arising from the logistics of "balancing" from the small number of essential actors or from the lack of flexibility of the "balancing" apparatus.[2]

It is apparent that Kaplan's specification of the conditions which may lead to the breakdown of the "balance-of-power" system is a very impressive achievement. At the same time, however, his very success in bold simplification and specification seems to have led him to lose sight of the fact that, apart from the conditions regarding informational inputs and capability changes, his set of destabilizing conditions does not offer any substantive addition to the very description of the balance-of-power system as given by him. In other words, I submit that the first two conditions regarding the behavioral orientation of an essential actor are basically derived from the essential behavioral rules of the balance-of-power system, while the last two regarding various "difficulties" logically follow from the definition of the "balance-of-power" system. Except "failures in informational inputs" and "capability changes [with] positive feedback," all the conditions listed by Kaplan as leading to the destabilization of the balance-of-power system are essentially tautological within the analytic framework of his own logical universe. It is as if Kaplan had constructed pathological theories by simply listing the symptoms of normal health negatively.

But surely the interesting question is not what constitutes a breakdown; it is rather what leads to a breakdown. If the latter is the question we want to answer, it will not do simply to say that an international system may break down because one of the essential actors does not behave itself properly, for we will still want to know what makes a national actor reject the prevailing norms of an existing international system and act in defiance of them. Indeed, a theory of international change is nothing if not a theory of the causes of system-destructive behavior on the part of essential actors. It is, therefore, most essential to ask the question: What propels a nation-state to pursue ends that are destructive to the existing international system? As will be made clear later in discussing the findings of our own historical investigation, an effort to answer such a question on the basis of empirical data will normally lead us to raise another related question: What is the normal pattern of response on the part of conservative states to the system-destructive actions of a revolutionary power? In sum, Kaplan's analysis is not so much invalid as insufficient. It does not even raise the relevant questions to their fullest extent, although as a tautological statement Kaplan's specification of a "derelict" actor, as it were, is certainly valid.

If Kaplan's analysis suffers from a degree of insufficiency, that is, the lack of sufficient empirical relevance, Rosecrance's theorizing suffers from a sort of overeagerness to exploit historical data. The four major determinants of the international system as identified by Rosecrance are not so much insufficient in describing an international system as they are logically underdeveloped. Although I would not seriously object to the use of Rosecrance's four determinants, "direction, control, resources, and capacity," I do not find his discussion of "direction," for instance, very illuminating. To be sure, Rosecrance is on safe ground when he asserts in discussing the role of "direction" that "extreme instability is correlated with ideological conflict; extreme stability is associated with ideological concord."[3] But to stop at such a statement, as Rosecrance actually does, is not so much to explain the actual process whereby international relations are destabilized by the impact of ideological factors as simply to identify at the most elementary level a connection of an unspecified kind between ideological factors and international stability. Surely the important question is not whether extreme ideological conflict is good or bad for international stability, but rather if it is bad, why it is so and at what point ideological heterogeneity becomes disruptive of international stability. My impression is that Rosecrance has failed to penetrate to the needed depth of careful and detailed analysis mainly because his overeagerness makes him try to use too much history all at once. As a consequence of his attempt to account for the entire history of modern international relations, he seems to have neglected the more critical need to look into the conditions of stability and the process of destabilization more carefully. Had he analyzed one recognizable international system more exhaustively rather than trying to encompass the entire history of modern international relations, he might have dealt with the questions that his list of basic determinants necessarily contains.

In the light of the above criticism of Kaplan's and Rosecrance's works, it is possible, I believe, to say that the grand ambition to formulate a general and comprehensive theory of international stability and its dissolution is not likely to prove easily realizable. I propose instead to offer a set of hypotheses that are neither exhaustive nor confirmed but that at least have the virtue of having been generated by the analysis of one historical example. The hypotheses that I have extracted from my historical analysis only partially explain the process of international destabilization in the sense that they do not exhaust all the conditions and factors which may contribute to the breakdown of an international system. I have not, for instance, dealt with the factors external to the international system, a drastic change among which is bound to affect the stability of a given system. For this reason, the following propositions which I submit for further empirical test constitute only a partial explanation for the phenomenon of international destabilization.

There is also another sense, however, in which I can say that my propositions are partial. I submit the following hypotheses in their present form because I am persuaded of the futility of a research strategy that tries to formulate a general, comprehensive, and exhaustive theory of international relations. Many things happen in international relations, and one does not have to have a comprehensive general theory to be able to discover and explain connections between one event or factor and another event or factor. Therefore, instead of trying to offer a total explanation of international destabilization, I have examined rather carefully one historical example of international-system breakdown and tried to find out what factors influenced international stability and how. As these findings are derived from one case study, there is no sense in pretending that their general validity has been proved. At the same time, it is reasonable to think that they may well be generally valid. To discover if this is really so or not is the task of further comparative studies, for which this book claims no more than to have laid a sort of groundwork. If and when they are confirmed to be generally valid, they can then be regarded as laws of international relations.

●   ●   ●

It will be recalled that the analysis presented in this book is based on the assumption that the stability of an international system depends on two things, i.e., limitation in the ends pursued by essential actors of the given system and limitation in the means employed to achieve those ends. This rather simple assumption has the virtue of helping us formulate certain crucial questions: What brings about drastic changes in the limited character of ends and means in international relations? How and why does a nation-state renounce traditional limits upon its aims and instruments of foreign policy? What factors are responsible for escalation in the stakes in international conflicts?

These are the questions that have been raised repeatedly in regard to the process of international relations of the period under study. Now some general answers can be attempted, and for the sake of clarity they are presented in the following schematic form.

Hypothesis I:

A heterogeneous ideology tends to reduce international stability by sharply increasing the probability of distortion in perception.

From Napoleon's contemptuous designation of his philosophical enemies as "ideologists" to Marx's identification of "ideology" with "false consciousness," the term *ideology* had an essentially polemical flavor. It was used to accuse one's political enemies of intentionally or unintentionally falsifying reality that was inconsistent with ideological formulations. The accused, of course, did not take the blame calmly. In fact, today the accusation of "ideology" in this sense is more effectively directed against the heirs of the Marxist dogma than its critics, who have somewhat surprisingly managed to celebrate the "end of ideology" for themselves. In any case, as far as world politics is concerned, the concept of ideology has been most frequently used to describe the expansionist policies of the enemies of Western democracies, although critics of American foreign policy too have tended to criticize it on the ground that it is more ideological ("legalistic-moralistic," etc.) than "realistic."

Ideological foreign policy, according to the polemical understanding of it, is that policy which pursues ends and objectives inconsistent with the reality of international relations. In other words, the primary relevance of ideological factors to international relations is assumed to lie in the clash of conscious objectives and ultimate values. The trouble with such an assumption is that it imputes to ideology at once too much and too little: too much if ideological differences are always assumed to constitute causes for international conflicts, and too little because viewing ideology only in terms of conscious objectives and ultimate values fails to sensitize us to the highly critical role that ideological commitment plays in the perceptual process of the ideologically committed. In other words, it is not warranted to say that ideological differences always lead to irreconcilable conflict. What a difference in ideology does is to put an additional strain on a given international system by sharply increasing the chances of international misunderstanding.

International relations can be regarded as a system of action, and insofar as this is true, international stability depends upon, among other things, the degree to which the actors of a given system share a common or compatible scheme of perception. Symbols, verbal and other kinds, which constitute the very stuff

through which nation-states interact with each other, can be perceived in more ways than one. It does not take a great imagination, therefore, to suspect that the degree of predictability will be
comparatively lower in a system in which actors interpret available symbols in different ways than it will be in a perceptually homogeneous system. It is precisely for this reason that the injection
of a heterogeneous ideology into a given international system will
normally lead to the lowering of predictability of international
behavior of ideologically heterogeneous actors and consequently
to instability of international relations in general.

To turn to the example at hand, the first and most obvious
incident that illustrates the proposition that is being suggested
here is the unexpected impact of the so-called "Pillnitz declaration," the influence of which upon the French people was exactly
the opposite of what its authors had anticipated. In the normal
practice of classical diplomacy, it would not have taken great in-
genuity to interpret correctly what was really meant by the well-
known conditional clause of the declaration. But the fact was that
the French were no longer attached to the normal practice of classical diplomacy. There had been ideological revolution in France,
and as a result the French tended to view the outside world in
radically different terms than before. The symbolic act of the conservative powers could not have the expected influence upon the
French people, because influence that is effective in accordance
with what Carl Friedrich has called "the rule of anticipated reaction"[4] presupposes a community of perception, a condition that
was certainly not present in the revolutionary period.

The point, however, is not only that the French misunder-
stood the intentions of the conservative signatories to the declaration, but equally critically, the conservative powers failed to
anticipate the probable reactions of a nation involved in a democratic revolution. When, for instance, the French offered to negotiate over the Alsace domain, the German princes seem to have
wrongly interpreted it as a sign of French weakness, which could
be cheaply turned into an easy capitulation. Later, when France,
through her own domestic evolution, came to pursue goals that
were basically destructive of the inherited international system,

the conservative actors again failed to perceive correctly the nature and implications of the threat posed by revolutionary France. By the same token, of course, France, now gaining at the expense of the conservative actors' failure of perception, conducted her own foreign policy on the basis of a similar misperception. She underrated the ultimate power of resistance which the conservative states were still capable of putting up against France's imperialistic drive, and simultaneously overrated the potential receptivity of the non-French peoples to the revolutionary message. In fact, if we look at the conflict between revolutionary France and conservative Europe in this light, it takes on the appearance of a Greek tragedy in which protagonists are blindly driven toward their inevitable mutual destruction through an uncontrollable fate based on some tragic flaw. The flaw in this case would be intellectual limitation.

To be sure, distorted perception is not exclusive to an ideologically heterogeneous international system. A community founded upon an ideological consensus also suffers not infrequently from contradictory schemes of perception that are inevitably present in it, insofar as it is a community of men and not angels. What makes the problem of distorted perception far more acute in an ideologically heterogeneous system compared to a homogeneous one is that, in the former, perceptual distortion is not only built into the system by virtue of conflicting ideological convictions, but also it is infinitely more difficult to overcome than in the latter situation. Miscalculations of mutual intent are essentially technical difficulties insofar as they arise between actors committed to a similar world-view, and as such they can be reduced to a more or less manageable proportion through heightened awareness of the problem. In contrast, distorted perception resulting from an ideological conviction is basically an integral part of the ideological commitment itself, which makes it quite impossible to "correct" the perceptual process short of either gradually or suddenly discarding the very ideological conviction that gave rise to the misunderstanding.

The reason is that ideology necessarily includes a view of "reality" as well as a commitment to values and goals. If only the latter were in question, perceptual distortion would still be a problem, but a conscious effort to eliminate it would go a long way toward reducing it to a tolerable degree. What renders futile even a conscious effort of an ideologically committed actor to free himself from perceptual distortion is the fact that his ideological commitment necessarily entails a set of propositions about the world of facts, the acceptance of which is bound to predispose him toward a certain interpretation of world events. An ideologically convinced actor, therefore, starts from an a priori conception of reality, and to the degree that there is bound to be some distance between reality as such and an ideological conception of it, an ideological conviction naturally results in distorted perception.

As has been suggested in the introduction, there may be a sense in which all thinking can be said to be ideological. This would be particularly true of political thought, insofar as political thought necessarily entails judgments about values and objectives. It is also true in the sense that thinking cannot be so completely empirical as to presume absolutely no a priori presupposition about the nature of reality. Does this then mean that since all thinking is ideological in essence, international relations too are always ideological and therefore unstable?

The answer is negative on two accounts. First, as I have already argued, the role of ideological factors in international relations should be understood in relational rather than substantive terms. The relevant point is not that foreign policies are expressions of ideologies basically but that international stability is affected by the degree to which actors in an international system share a common ideology or at least hold compatible beliefs and values. The reason for this is that ideology affects international relations mainly through the perceptual process. Second, there are obviously degrees of strength or rigidity in ideological convictions, making some belief systems more difficult to modify or discard than others. Even in a case of the same ideological beliefs, the strength of conviction is not uniform from one believer to another. One may more easily adapt to changes in objective circumstances than another who, with his perception frozen into an absolute conviction, often fails to recognize even the fact of change.

International stability, then, is not only affected by the content of competing ideologies, but also varies inversely with the degree of rigidity in ideological conviction. In a confrontation of ideologically heterogeneous actors, it makes a difference whether the actors are capable of transcending the perceptual limitations of their ideological belief systems or not. The more capable they are of doing so, the more they are likely to succeed in minimizing the disruptive effect of their ideological differences upon their relations. To borrow Anatol Rapaport's distinctions, ideological flexibility makes for "debates" whereas rigidity tends to lead to "fights" and "games,"[5] and debates, even when accompanied by occasional fights, are more condusive to stable international relations than "games" with fixed and rigid goals. In sum, it can be stated that international destabilization is a function of (1) the degree of ideological rigidity and (2) the extent of ideological heterogeneity. Hypothesis I shows why this is the case.

Hypothesis II:

The emergence of an antisystemic foreign policy in a revolutionary state is a function of interaction between the revolutionary domestic condition of the state and its international predicament.

Ordinarily, the antisystemic behavior of a state has been explained in terms of its basic "goal" orientation. Thus, for instance, textbooks in international relations abound in such expressions as "satiated" versus "unsatiated," "revisionist" versus "status quo," or "imperialistic" versus "conservative" states. These familiar expressions are meaningful and descriptive as far as they go, but they ignore the *source* of the behavior characteristic of states thus described. A state acts in a "revisionist" or antisystemic manner not simply out of some internally generated ambition but more often as a result of interaction between the state's internal condition and its external situation. To be sure, the relative weight of internal and external factors varies from country to country and from one historical period to another. It depends, for instance, on geography, population, historical tradition, and so on.

We can say as a general rule, however, that foreign policy is always influenced to some degree by the effect of external circumstances on domestic development. This, I believe, is particularly true of a revolutionary state that pursues goals destructive of the status quo. Therefore, I argue in Hypothesis II that first, a revolutionary state does not automatically pursue antisystemic goals in its foreign policy, and second, whether it actually does so or not depends on the effect of the existing international system upon the domestic political structure. In other words, the road from an ideological revolution within to a war against the existing system of international relations is neither an automatic nor a straight route. What often moves a nation along the road is its international predicament.

Thus, for instance, the Revolution of 1789 did not automatically predispose France to a revolutionary foreign policy. On the contrary, if the Revolution had any immediate effect on French foreign policy, it was to put a brake on the traditional Bourbon drive. Conscious of its isolation, and distrustful of its own monarchy, France of 1789 was timid in its external posture if only out of the inevitable lack of self-confidence that charcterizes a revolutionary regime. What turned France from an essentially defensive concern to a policy of universal liberation of "oppressed" peoples was, in the first place, the advent of the Girondin party which advocated a revolutionary foreign policy, and in the second place, the attitude of conservative powers which had in no small measure helped to bring about a situation in France that led to the triumph of the war party. The ideological universalism that characterized the expansionist phase of French foreign policy was not alien to the spirit of 1789, but it was one thing to have within France a few who talked in terms of a missionary obligation to rid Europe of the "tyrants," and quite another to have their program of action accepted as a national policy. The cause of the transformation from one to the other, I maintain, was a series of events that happened in France's external relations rather than in her domestic sphere. Had the conservative powers been willing to accept revolutionary France as a respectable member of European society and to refrain from all gestures that could be construed as threats to the basic security and indeed the very survival of revolutionary France, the chances are that the party of war and universalistic foreign policy might not have prevailed in France. Consequently, French foreign policy might very well have remained moderate, sober, and consistent with the requirements of the traditional international system.

The reason for the emergence of a system-destructive policy then is that the system fails to function adequately to guarantee the minimum security of an ideologically revolutionary actor. It is because of such failure that a revolutionary state is most likely to reject the system, and not necessarily because of any conviction that the given international system is unjust. Although the latter conviction is frequently held by a revolutionary actor, it is highly doubtful that any state will actually act upon it, unless it is persuaded that the entire system is opposed to its very existence. When the behavior of conservative states creates the impression that the revolutionary state has no choice but between total rejection of the existing international system and its own destruction by the system, the probability is very high that the struggle for power within the revolutionary state will end in the triumph of the party that identifies the national interest with some transnational goal destructive of the international system. When that happens, the dice are cast for the unlimited struggle between ideologically committed enemies. The "war" has become ideological, and "total."

Hypothesis III:

> The response of conservative states to an emergent revolutionary state is a function of the nature of the existing international system.

Hypothesis II has highlighted the extent to which the behavior of conservative states is responsible for maintaining international stability. Hypothesis III states that the manner in which they are likely to behave toward a new revolutionary state is largely determined by the pattern of behavior characteristic of the system in which they are conservative actors. Indeed conservative states would not be conservative unless their behavior were pat-

terned after the normative requirements of an inherited system.
There is, therefore, nothing surprising in the discovery that a conservative response to an ideologically divergent actor is determined by the nature of a given system of action.

The truth of the above hypothesis was seen in the record of
the Coalition's dismal failure in its struggle against revolutionary
France. Confronted with a challenge the novelty of which was not
anticipated by the conservative mind, the crowned rulers of Europe acted as if nothing of revolutionary proportion had really
occurred to the classical balance-of-power system. Despite their
occasional rhetoric, their more serious concern seems not to have
been with the fundamental threat posed by the ideological revolution in France, but rather with concrete territorial gains and
economic advantages. That they should have remained almost
obstinately attached to the pursuit of tangible and limited goals is
of course consistent with the nature of the system to which they
had been accustomed. It is, however, true that their failure to rise
above the limits of the traditional system contributed in no small
measure to the survival and indeed the very military success of
revolutionary France.

If the pattern of conservative response to a revolutionary
state is essentially a function of the traditional international system, it also stands to reason that some international systems will
be inherently more stable than others. Those systems that are inherently more stable conceivably contain certain built-in features
which more easily alert conservative actors to the problem of dealing with a revolutionary challenge. In this regard, the eighteenth-
century balance-of-power system was basically less stable than the
restored system that came afterwards, since the latter was founded
on a conscious attempt to establish and maintain such a system,
while the former was relatively spontaneous and lacking in self-
consciousness.[6] It is also conceivable that, other things being
equal, a hierarchically structured system may be more stable than
a "balance-of-power" system, which is a prototype of an international system based on the principle of equality. In the former
case, any deviating actor would constitute an easily recognizable
challenge to the principle of hierarchy, whereas in the latter case

the very principle of equality tends to obscure the revolutionary character of an actor that is ideologically different from the rest.

It goes without saying that conservative states will be better able to cope with the emergence of a revolutionary state as their understanding of the implications of the latter phenomenon increases. It is, perhaps, for this reason that a balance-of-power system, which places such a great premium on the egoism of a state, is generally ill suited for a revolutionary age. In the face of ideological heterogeneity, it does not seem to be enough for conservative states to concern themselves exclusively with their own petty and tangible interests. The need to transcend the limits of ordinary life can never be greater than in a revolutionary age.

Hypothesis III, however, does not mean that the best response toward an emergent revolutionary state is necessarily one of transcendental hostility. Overcoming the routine does not automatically result in a counterrevolutionary crusade. Indeed, if we combine the insights of Hypotheses II and III, the most viable response to an ideologically dissimilar state may more likely be a combination of a willingness to accept the state in question as a regular member of the international system, and a resolve to unite with other conservative states in a common effort to deal with the revolutionary actor. As has been pointed out, however, such a response depends on the nature of a given international system. Obviously the intellectual and imaginative capacity required for such a response is quite frequently absent in international life.

Hypothesis IV:

> The probability of a breakdown of a given international system varies directly with (1) the extent of ideological heterogeneity, (2) the degree of ideological rigidity among the essential actors, and (3) the strength of the feedback effect of the divergent actor's international action on its domestic political system; and inversely with (4) the amount of "security" enjoyed by the ideologically divergent actor, and (5) the degree of "system" orientation in the traditional international system.

Hypothesis IV is an attempt to combine the insights of previous hypotheses in an effort to formulate a general theory of international-system breakdown. The variables linked with the probability of a system breakdown are derived from the propositions submitted as Hypotheses I to III. It has already been noted that they can be only provisional since they are generated essentially through one historical case study. More important, it should be borne in mind that Hypothesis IV is not intended to offer an exhaustive list of the significant variables for the explanation of radical destabilization in international relations. I have not dealt with important ecological factors which certainly can affect the level of stability in a given international system. Rather, my aim has been to concentrate on *action*, and it will be noted that the principal emphasis of Hypothesis IV is upon the behavioral pattern of international actors rather than the environmental factors affecting them. This emphasis on the analysis of action does not indicate that I minimize the weight of environmental factors. On the contrary, it is my view that environmental factors need a separate and detailed analysis before one can begin to incorporate them along with action-related variables into a coherent and general theory of international stability.

As for the variables themselves, there is no need here for extensive comment. Items 1 and 2 are derived from Hypothesis I, while item 3 is suggested by Hypothesis II. By the strength of "feedback effect," I mean to indicate the degree to which a state's international involvement can influence both the process and the outcome of its domestic politics. Calling it "feedback effect" reminds us of the interactive nature of the relationship between international and domestic systems. What item 3 suggests is that the more vulnerable a nation's domestic political life is to the influence of the international situation, the more likely an ideologically divergent state will be to undergo a radical transformation of its domestic political system. This seems to be the case because ideological heterogeneity in itself guarantees a certain degree of international isolation and hostility, which then tends to react upon the domestic situation to the extent to which the political system is sensitive to the influences of international development.

In our example, the war of 1792 can be said to have had a feed-back effect in that the so-called "Second Revolution" was to a great extent a function of what happened in the war. The Second Revolution, which was a further radicalization of France's domestic political life, led in turn to the emergence of revolutionary foreign policy. . . .

Item 4 is certainly related to item 3 since both variables have to do with the process of the emergence of system-destructive policy. The former has the virtue of singling out one specific condition that can radically influence the goal orientation of an ideologically divergent state. It asserts that the more insecure a nation with dissimilar ideology feels in a given international system, the more likely it will be to define its international goals in terms antithetic to the requirements of that system. If this is true, the normative implications are enormous, for the essence of conservative statesmanship then becomes one of persuading a revolutionary state that no radical rearrangement of the existing international framework is needed for it to enjoy its minimal "security." To be sure, such a task may be an impossible one to accomplish under certain circumstances. A revolutionary state may have already convinced itself of its insecurity so strongly that no amount of effort on the part of conservative states may make any difference. It seems to me, however, that to the degree the foreign policy of a country depends on the outcome of its political process, it is unwise to assume too great a finality—too easily—too often—in international relations. There remains always a margin of changeability in a nation's external posture. If item 4 is valid, then international stability depends to a very great extent on the willingness and ability of conservative states to act in such a way as to guarantee the security of a revolutionary state. "Appeasement" may not always be a dirty word after all.

There is, however, a difference between acting consciously to convince an ideologically revolutionary state of its basic security, on the one hand, and failing to threaten it simply by not recognizing the challenge that it necessarily poses to the traditional international system. The latter derives from the basic inertia of a conservative system, while the former presupposes a sophisticated intellectual flexibility. What course of response to the appearance of a revolutionary state a conservative state will choose depends, among other things, on the nature of the inherited international system. If the traditional system of international relations has predisposed conservative actors to the pursuit of their short-range goals without any consciousness of the systemic dimension of international life, the most likely pattern of conservative response will be to minimize the novelty of a revolutionary state and its destabilizing potential. In such a case, conservative states will act very "normally" within the framework of the traditional international system. If they do not mount an authentic counterrevolutionary attack, it is not because of their realization of the truth about the relation of "security" to moderation in a revolutionary state, but rather because they have failed to recognize the novelty of the new situation.

This, it will be recalled, was the case in our historical example, as the analysis of the failure of the First Coalition indicated. The conservative allies remained completely attached to the traditional pursuit of petty and divisive objectives at the expense of acting effectively against revolutionary France—and this failure to appreciate the newness of the new and act accordingly was essentially due to the nature of the international system under the old regime. The classical balance-of-power system of the eighteenth century had lacked the necessary "system" orientation. The self-centered dynastic states were so committed to the pursuit of territorial and other tangible gains that they were not prepared to recognize the less tangible challenge of heterogeneous ideology. As if out of youthful innocence, they tended to take for granted the "systemic" foundation of their rivalries and competitions without which the very essence of their international life, that is, the limited character of their conflicts and pursuits, would have been unthinkable. This tendency to remain unconscious of the systemic dimension of their interstate relations had foredoomed the conservative states to an uncreative response toward the revolutionary state—and its inevitable failure.

Item 5 alerts us to this connection between the nature of the traditional international system and the success or failure of conservative states in dealing with the challenge of a revolutionary state. If this connection is established, it will mean that the level of statesmanship that can be expected of any conservative power in a revolutionary age is by and large limited by the structure of the traditional system itself. Only to the extent that conservative statesmen can free themselves intellectually from the compulsions of the traditional system, can they be expected to act with flexibility, which is the minimal quality needed for dealing with the problem of a revolutionary state. Neither automatic hostility nor innocent indifference can be a viable response to the emergence of an ideologically revolutionary power. Oddly enough, it seems that the chances of maintaining the stability of a traditional international system are in the last analysis dependent upon the ability of conservative actors to transcend the constraints of that system.

Notes

1. Morton A. Kaplan, *System and Process in International Politics* (New York, 1957). Richard N. Rosecrance, *op. cit.*

2. Morton A. Kaplan, *op. cit.*, p. 23.

3. Richard N. Rosecrance, *op. cit.*, pp. 280–281.

4. Carl J. Friedrich, *Constitutional Government and Politics* (New York, 1937), pp. 16–17.

5. Anatol Rapaport, *Fights, Games and Debates* (Ann Arbor, Mich., 1960).

6. A similar point has been made by some historians who saw the concert as an improvement upon the eighteenth-century balance-of-power system. See, for example, Leonce Donadieu, *Essai sur la théorie de l'équilibre* (Paris, 1900), and Charles Dupuis, *Le Principe d'équilibre et le concert européen* (Paris, 1909).

Bibliography

I. French Sources

Arneth, A. R. von, ed., *Marie Antoinette, Joseph II und Leopold II: Ihr Briefwechsel*, Leipzig, 1866.
> Contains letters by de Mercy as well as some by Louis XVI. Useful on the origins of the war.

Aulard, F. A., ed., *Recueil des actes du comité salut public avec la correspondance officielle des représentants en mission et le registre du conseil executif provisoire*, 28 vols., Paris, 1889-1951.
> Useful on the Convention and the Committee of Public Safety.

Brissot, J.-P., *Correspondance et papiers*, Paris, 1919.

Buchez, P.-J.-B., and P.-C. Roux, *Histoire parlementaire de la Révolution française, ou Journal des assemblées nationales depuis 1789 jusqu'en 1815*, 40 vols., Paris, 1834-1838.
> Includes many things besides parliamentary debates.

Charavay, E., ed., *Correspondance général de Carnot*, 4 vols., Paris, 1892-1907.

Debidour, A., ed., *Recueil des actes du Directoire executif*, 4 vols., Paris, 1910–1917.
> Useful on the Directory, but less convenient than Aulard's collection as it lacks an index.

Fribourg, A., ed., *Discours de Danton*, Paris, 1910.

Kaulek, J., ed., *Papiers de Barthélemy, ambassadeur de France en Suisse, 1792-1797*, 6 vols., Paris, 1886-1910.
> The instructions Barthélemy received from Paris are very revealing.

Mavidal, J., E. Laurent, *et al.*, *Archives parlementaires, recueil complet des débats législatifs et politiques des Chambres françaises de 1787 à 1860*, Ser. I, 1787-1799, 82 vols., Paris, 1868-1892.

More reliable than the collection by Buchez and Roux, but
also more limited in coverage. A very convenient index.

Reimpression de l'ancien Moniteur, 31 vols., Paris, 1858-1870.
Le Moniteur universel was the best newspaper during the
Revolution. This reprint is indispensable and convenient.
The last two volumes are indexes.

Vellay, C., *Discours et rapports de Robespierre,* Paris, 1908.

Wormeley, K. P., ed. and trans., *Diary and Correspondence of
Count Axel Fersen, Grand-Marshal of Sweden, Relating to the
Court of France,* Boston, 1902.
Useful on the origins of the war.

II. British Sources

Cambridge History of British Foreign Policy, The, 1783-1919,
Vol. I, Cambridge, 1939.
Appendixes, pp. 543-602, contain many essential materials.

Great Britain Historical Manuscripts Commission, *Report on the
Manuscripts of J. B. Fortescue, Esq.,* 10 vols., London,
1892-1927.
Called "Dropmore Papers" because the manuscripts are
housed at Dropmore. Contains the official correspondence of
Lord Grenville, Pitt's foreign secretary from 1791 to 1805.
Also includes the reports of various secret agents to the Secretary and the correspondence of special envoys such as Malmesbury as well as regular diplomatists.

Bath and Wells, The Bishop of, ed., with an introduction, *The
Journal and Correspondence of William, Lord Auckland,* 4
vols. London, 1861-1862.

Malmesbury, The Third Earle of, ed., *Diaries and Correspondence of James Harris, First Earle of Malmesbury,* 4 vols., London, 1844-1845.
Indispensable for Malmesbury's negotiations.

III. German Sources

Hansen, J., ed., *Quellen zur Geschichte des Rheinlandes im zeitalter der französischen Revolution, 1780-1801,* 4 vols., Bonn,
1931-1938.
More inclusive in coverage than the title indicates. Very conveniently arranged with indexes and notes.

Huffer, H., ed., *Quellen zur Geschichte des zeitalters der französ-*

ischen Revolution, Part II, Vol. I (ed. by F. Luckwaldt), Innsbruck, 1907.
   May be used to supplement the Vivenot collection.

Ranke, Leopold von, *Ursprung und Beginn der Revolutionskriege, 1791-1792,* Leipzig, 1875.
   Analekten 4 and 5 are useful sources.

Vivenot, A. R. von, and H. von Zeissberg, *Quellen zur Geschichte der deutschen Kaiserpolitik Oesterreichs während der französischen Revolutionskriege,* 5 vols. (I and II by Vivenot and III to V by Zeissberg), Vienna, 1873–1890.
   Very useful and convenient, but covers the period only to September, 1795.

Books

I. History

Adams, E. D., *The Influence of Grenville on Pitt's Foreign Policy,* Washington, 1904.

Beloff, Max, *The Age of Absolution, 1660-1815,* New York, 1962.

Biro, S. S., *The German Policy of Revolutionary France,* 2 vols., Cambridge, Mass., 1957.
   An extensively documented study, but clearly prejudiced against the Revolution.

Bourgeois, E., *Manuel historique de politique étrangère,* 4 vols., Paris, 1945–49, Vol. II (1789–1930).

Brinton, Crane, *A Decade of Revolution, 1789-1799,* New York, 1934.

Chuquet, A., *Les Guerres de la Révolution,* 11 vols., Paris, 1886-1896.
   Broadly conceived, more than a history of battles. Still very useful.

Clapham, J. H., *The Causes of the War of 1792,* Cambridge, England, 1899.

Dorn, Walter L., *Competition for Empire, 1740-1763,* New York 1940.

Dumolin, M., *Précis d'histoire militaire,* 2 vols., Paris, 1901-1912.

Earle, E. M., ed., *Makers of Modern Strategy,* Princeton, 1944.

Fugier, A., *Histoire des relations internationales,* Vol. IV: *La Révolution française et l'Empire napoléonienne,* Paris, 1954.

Godechot, J. L., *La Grande Nation: L'expansion révolutionnaire de la France dans le mode de 1789 à 1799*, 2 vols., Paris, 1956.
A well-known and very scholarly work. Along with R. R. Palmer's work, Godechot's book sees the revolutionary expansion as a product of the concurrently widespread revolutionary situation rather than French national power.

————, *La Contre-révolution: Doctrine et action, 1789-1804*, Paris, 1961.

Goetz-Bernstein, H. A., *La Diplomatie de la Gironde, Jacques-Pierre Brissot,* Paris, 1912.
Scholarly and indispensable.

Guyot, R., *Le Directoire et la paix de l'Europe des traités de Bale à la Deuxiemme Coalition* (1795–1799), Paris, 1911.
An indispensable reading; "corrects" many of Sorel's interpretations.

Heriot, A., *The French in Italy, 1796-1799*, London, 1957.

Jomini, Henri, *Histoire critique et militaire des guerres de la Révolution*, 15 vols., Paris, 1819–1824.

Lavisse, E., ed., *Histoire de France contemporaine depuis la Révolution jusqu'à la paix de 1919*, 9 vols., Paris, 1920-1922, Vol. II: G. Pariset, *La Révolution, 1792-1799*.

Lefebvre, G., *La Révolution française*, 2e édition, Paris, 1951; Vol. XIII of L. Halphen and P. Sagnac, eds., *Peuples et civilizations: Histoire générale*, 20 vols., Paris, 1928–1939.
Available in English translation as *The French Revolution from Its Origins to 1793*, translated by Elizabeth Moss Evanson, and *The French Revolution: From 1793 to 1799*, translated by John H. Stewart and James Friguglietti, London and New York, 1962-1964.

Lord, R. H., *The Second Partition of Poland, A Study in Diplomatic History*, Cambridge, Mass., 1915.

Mahan, A. T., *Influence of Sea Power upon the French Revolution and Empire, 1793-1813*, 10th edition, New York, 1898.

Masson, F., *Le Ministere des affaires étrangeres pendant la Révolution, 1787-1804*, Paris, 1877.

Mathiez, A., *Danton et la paix,* Paris, 1919.
Heavily prejudiced against Danton, whom, with the benefit of hindsight, we may be more inclined to see as a shining oasis of pragmatism in a dizzy revolutionary inferno. Danton's foreign policy merits a second look.

_____, *La Réaction thermidoreanne,* Paris, 1929.

Navonne, B., *La Diplomatie du Directoire et Bonaparte d'après les papiers inedits de Reubell,* Paris, 1951.
Scholarly and useful.

Nussbaum, F. L., *The Triumph of Science and Reason, 1660–1685,* New York, 1953.

Palmer, R. R., *The Age of the Democratic Revolution, A Political History of Europe and America, 1760-1800,* 2 vols., Princeton, 1959–1964.
An excellent synthesis; makes the same argument as Godechot's thesis about the "Atlantic revolution."

Rain, P., *La Diplomatie française de Mirabeau à Bonaparte,* Paris, 1950.

Roberts, Penfield, *The Quest for Security, 1715–1740,* New York, 1947.

Rohden, P. R., *Die Klassische Diplomatie, von Kaunitz bis Metternich,* Leipzig, 1939.

Rose, J. H., *William Pitt and the Great War,* London, 1911.

Rudé, G., *The Crowd in the French Revolution,* Oxford, 1959.

Sagnac, P., *Le Rhin français pendant la Révolution et l'Empire,* Paris, 1917.

Seton-Watson, R. W., *Britain in Europe, 1789–1914,* Cambridge, England, 1927.

Soboul, A., *Les soldats de l'an II,* Paris, 1959.

Sorel, A., *L'Europe et la Révolution française,* 9th edition, 8 vols., Paris, 1905.
Monumental is the word. Indispensable but its basic interpretation is equally unacceptable to this author.

Sybel, Heinrich von, *Geschichte der Revolutionszeit,* 10 vols., revised, Stuttgart, 1867-1869. English translation: *History of the French Revolution,* translated by Walter C. Perry, 4 vols., London, 1897–1900.
A monumental treatise, marred by Sybel's inability to conceal discreetly his anti-French and anti-Austrian prejudices.

Sydenham, M. J., *The Girondins,* London, 1961.

Tassier, Suzanne, *Histoire de la Belgique sous l'occupation française en 1792 et 1793,* Brussels, 1934.

Wahl, A., *Geschichte des europäischen Staatensystems im Zeitalter der französischen Revolution and der Freiheitzkriege, 1789–1815,* München, 1912.

Less monumental than the works of Sybel and Sorel, but equally valuable for the international situation of the period.

Walter, G., *Robespierre*, 2nd edition, Paris, 1946.

Ward, A. W., and G. P. Gooch, *The Cambridge History of British Foreign Policy*, 3 vols., Cambridge, 1922–1923.
Volume I, covering the period from 1783 to 1815, was reprinted in 1939 and remains indispensable.

Wilkinson, S., *The French Army Before Napoleon*, Oxford, 1915.

Wolf, J. B., *The Emergence of the Great Powers, 1685–1715*, New York, 1951.

II. Theory

Aron, R., *Paix et guerre entre les nations*, Paris, 1962.

Carr, E. H., *The Twenty Years' Crisis, 1919–1939*, London, 1940.

Claude, I. L., Jr., *Power and International Relations*, New York, 1962.

Herz, J. H., *International Politics in the Atomic Age*, New York, 1959.

Hoffmann, S., ed., *Contemporary Theory in International Relations*, Englewood Cliffs, N. J., 1960.

———, *The State of War: Essays in the Theory and Practice of International Politics*, New York, 1965.

Kaplan, M. A., *System and Process in International Politics*, New York, 1957.

Morgenthau, H. J., *Politics Among Nations, The Struggle for Power and Peace*, New York, 1960.

Ranke, Leopold, "The Great Powers," in Theodore H. von Laue, *Leopold Ranke: The Formative Years*, Princeton, 1950.

Rosecrance, R. N., *Action and Reaction in World Politics: International Systems in Perspective*, Boston, 1963.

Schiffer, W., *The Legal Community of Mankind*, New York, 1954.

Index

144